W9-CQA-512

Augustus Earle

Travel Artist

Augustus Earle

Travel Artist

Paintings and drawings in the
Rex Nan Kivell Collection
National Library of Australia

by
Jocelyn Hackforth-Jones

Scolar Press, London

First published in Australia 1980 by
the National Library of Australia,
Canberra
First published in Great Britain 1980
by Scolar Press, 90/91 Great Russell
Street, London WC1B 3PY
© National Library of Australia 1980
ISBN 0 85967 631 5
Printed in Australia

Preface

The National Library of Australia is the fortunate possessor of a large number of paintings and drawings by Augustus Earle (1793-1838), the London-born artist whose adventurous life encompassed travels to South America, Australia, New Zealand, the Pacific Islands, Southeast Asia and India, an enforced sojourn of eight months as a castaway on Tristan da Cunha, and a voyage in the *Beagle* during which he befriended the young Charles Darwin.

The major part of the Library's collection of 168 original pictures by or attributed to Earle is a series of 161 watercolours and drawings depicting places that he visited on his travels, and including a number of portraits and shipboard scenes. This series was acquired in 1959 from Mr (later Sir) Rex Nan Kivell (1898-1977), the New Zealand-born art dealer of the Redfern Gallery, London, whose unrivalled private collection of pictures, manuscripts and printed material relating to Australia, New Zealand and the Pacific has so greatly enriched the National Library. The series of 161 works had been originally in the possession of Admiral William Henry Smyth, the artist's half-brother; it passed in due course to the admiral's grandson, Herbert Warington Smyth, on whose behalf it was auctioned by Sotheby & Co. in London in May 1926. The catalogue note says, in part, 'These well-finished Water-colour Drawings were probably made with the idea of their publication as coloured aquatints, possibly while the artist was sailing the Southern Seas in the Gunboat commanded by his stepbrother [sic] Capt. (afterwards Admiral) Smyth. The whole Collection is mounted in an old folio scrapbook, 19in. by 13in.'

The collection was bought at Sotheby's for £1,800 by the dealer Walter Spencer, from whom it was later purchased, 'at an enhanced value', by Rex Nan Kivell. With much other material, the 161 works by Earle were placed in the custody of the National Library by Nan Kivell in 1948; formal transfer to Australian ownership was completed in 1959. At the time when they came to the National Library, the watercolours were no longer in a scrapbook but separately mounted.

Of the seven other works by or attributed to Earle that are held in the National Library, six are also in the Rex Nan Kivell Collection, including all five of the oils. The Library's only other Earle, an attributed watercolour, is in the Petherick Collection; it is no. 168 in the plates of this book.

Because of the importance of this collection, its worldwide scope, and its considerable appeal to historical and artistic interest, the National Library commissioned and now publishes the study that follows. It does so in accordance with an expressed policy of the National Library Council that the Library should share as fully as possible with scholars, students and the general public the original manuscripts, fascinating pictorial records, rare books, and valuable literary, historical and social material in its collections. The author of the work, Jocelyn Hackforth-Jones, had made a study of Earle while an honours student of Professor Bernard Smith, F.S.A., F.A.H.A., in the Power Institute of Fine Arts, University of Sydney. The Library gratefully acknowledges Professor Smith's interest in the undertaking, and the enthusiasm for it of Dr Ursula Hoff, O.B.E., F.A.H.A., sometime Assistant Director of the National Gallery of Victoria, who was a member of the National Library Council when the study was first proposed.

The National Library will be grateful for any information that might add to its knowledge about Augustus Earle, or of the whereabouts of other works by him.

G. CHANDLER
Director-General
National Library of Australia
April 1980

Contents

Acknowledgments

This study is greatly indebted to Dr E. H. McCormick, of Auckland, whose pioneering work on Earle is incorporated in his introduction to Earle's *Narrative of a Residence in New Zealand* and *Journal of a Residence in Tristan da Cunha* (1966). The doctoral thesis of Professor Harold Spencer, formerly of Occidental College, Los Angeles, and now of the University of Connecticut, 'Augustus Earle: a Study of Early Nineteenth Century Travel Art and its Place in English Landscape and Genre Traditions' (Harvard, 1967), was also a most valuable source of information. Closer to home, I wish to express my acknowledgments and thanks to Eve Buscombe of the Power Institute of Fine Arts, University of Sydney, for her M.A. thesis, 'Artists and Their Sitters: a Colonial Portrait; a Guide to the Portrait Painters of New South Wales and Van Diemen's Land, 1820-1850' (Australian National University, 1970).

My special thanks are due to Professor Bernard Smith, first Power Professor of Contemporary Art and Director of the Power Institute of Fine Arts, University of Sydney, for reading the manuscript in its early unwieldy stages and for his patience in providing constructive criticism and consistently showing an interest in the work. Dr Ursula Hoff and Mary Mackay read and criticised the Introduction in an early draft; I am grateful for their help.

J.H-J.

Introduction

The first three decades of the nineteenth century were significant years in the history of travel art. While recent explorations had opened up vast new territories, these new lands were still unfamiliar to the man at home, whose appetite had been whetted by both written and verbal descriptions. As there was yet no photographic art, and as international travel was still slow and inefficient,[1] the man at home suffered feelings of isolation and frustration. The travel artist, then, occupied a unique position, and his paintings or published views, conjuring up an impression of these distant places, were greatly in demand and were highly prized by their purchasers.

Earle's life and the source of his style

Augustus Earle was probably the first professionally trained freelance travel artist to tour the world. Artists before him all appear to have embarked on voyages with commissions. Travel artists were either employed as draughtsmen on voyages of exploration, or were privately financed by individual patrons, often wealthy noblemen who, wishing to take home views of the places they had visited, included in their retinue an artist like William Alexander (1767-1816), who journeyed to Peking with Count Macartney. Artists who relied on this type of patronage included Thomas and William Daniell; with the financial support of their patron in England, they travelled to China and India with the purpose of publishing a book of aquatints (one of which was *Oriental Scenery*, 1795-1816). Some, like George Chinnery (1774-1852), preferred to settle in a particular country, relying on the patronage of the local aristocracy. Chinnery, a portrait painter, lived in China and India for fifty years. In 1815 the French artist Jean-Baptiste Debret (1768-1848) travelled to Brazil to establish a painting academy, and remained there as the official court painter.

Freed from the limiting constraints of this artist-patron relationship, Earle was able to indulge his love of travelling and explore the world at will, visiting a variety of different lands. He was not pressed continually to produce work for an employer, and was therefore able to settle in any place he fancied. He remained long enough to capture the very essence of life there. Earle's passion for travelling began at an early age and lasted throughout his life. His skill in recording what he saw and in instilling into the recorded image something of the life force of that place, together with his choice of unusual and diverse subject matter, is evident throughout his painting.

Earle's family background included two noted artists whose associations were with the new world rather than the old. He was the son of an American Tory, James Earl,[2] an American portrait painter who fled to England in 1778. In 1789, he married Caroline Smyth (the widow of an American Tory,

---

1 Photography was first introduced in 1841. Transatlantic steam travel was in general use after 1839.
2 Augustus later added a final 'e' to the family name.

Joseph Smyth) in London. In that year Earl was admitted to the Royal Academy and exhibited there in 1787-9. His brother, Ralph Earl, was an eminent portrait painter who had travelled to London in 1783 and studied under Benjamin West at the Royal Academy, exhibiting there until 1786. Augustus Earle had two older sisters. Phoebe (born in 1790)[3] was also an artist, a painter of fruit and flower pieces, and received an appointment as flower painter to the Queen. The second daughter, Clara, about whom little is known, was born in 1791 or 1792. On 1 June 1793 the youngest child, Augustus, was born at 54 Newman Street, London. He was only three when his father, who had travelled to America on business, died in Charleston of yellow fever.

Young Augustus seems to have displayed a talent for painting at an early age. He was only thirteen in 1806, when he exhibited *Judgement of Midas* (after Ovid; location unknown) at the Royal Academy, and until 1815 he exhibited there continually. He later became friendly with the school of young American painters studying in London from around 1811 (the year Morse, Leslie and Washington Allston arrived in England).[4] Together with Morse and Leslie, Earle visited the studio of a fellow-American, Benjamin West, who was noted for his generous patronage of young American artists, and who was at that time President of the Royal Academy. Earle probably took lessons at the Academy, but was not formally enrolled there.[5] Some sort of formal training however is indicated by his Academy exhibits from 1806 to 1815; these paintings follow progressively the usual range of accepted subject matter.[6]

Earle's preference for naturalistic studies and his penchant for investigating unfamiliar regions is first documented in 1813, when Samuel Morse related to William Dunlap the details of his sketching 'ramble' with Earle around Deal: 'With their sketchbooks and drawing apparatus, they visited the seashore and the towns adjacent, making pedestrian excursions into the country in search of scenery, and sometimes meeting an adventure.'[7] Earle's taste for adventure and travel further manifested itself in 1815 when he gained a passage on a storeship bound for Malta. This decision was doubtless influenced by the occasion of the marriage of his half-brother Captain (later

3 She married Denis Dighton, a printer who made engravings after some of Earle's drawings.

4 Samuel F. B. Morse is better known today as the inventor of the Morse Code. However, he was also the principal founder and president of the National Academy of Design in New York. He painted portraits from 1815, the year he opened a studio. Washington Allston was a popular painter of portraits and Biblical landscapes. His work is little known outside the United States. Although Charles Robert Leslie's paintings were in demand during his lifetime, today he is better known for his biography of John Constable.

5 Augustus Earle, *Narrative of a Residence in New Zealand and Journal of a Residence in Tristan da Cunha*, ed. E. H. McCormick (London: Oxford University Press, 1966), p.4.

6 The following paintings were exhibited at the Academy before Earle left for the United States in 1818.
1808 *Battle of Poitiers* (location unknown)
1809 *Caius Marcius taking Possession of the City of Corioli* (location unknown)
1811 *Banditti* (location unknown)
1812 *Banditti* (location unknown)
1814 *A Man-of-War's Boats Cutting out a French Barque* (location unknown)
1815 *View of the Harbour and Part of the Town of Calais* (private collection)

7 William Dunlap, *History of the Rise and Progress of the Arts of Design in the United States.* 3 vols. 3rd ed. (New York: Benjamin Blom, 1965), v.3, p.104.

Scudding before a heavy Gale off the
Cape, Lat. 44° (no. 54; 1824)

Admiral) W. H. Smyth to Annarella Warington at Messina. At any rate, he spent the next two years travelling in the Mediterranean — some of the time in Smyth's gunboat. He visited Malta at least twice and presumably made the preparatory sketches for the aquatint of the *Grand Harbour of Valetta* (private collection) during these visits. Earle must have shared his half-brother's interest in antiquities, for in 1816 they visited the ruins of Leptis Magna, where he painted his watercolour of the ruined city (now in the Royal Collection, Windsor Castle). In January 1817, Smyth returned to begin excavating the city, whilst Earle '. . . returned to Malta, passed through Sicily, and ascended Mount AEtna. He next proceeded to Gibraltar, taking a minute survey of that mighty rock, its batteries, caves, and Moorish ruins.'[8]

Scarcely had Earle arrived back in England (in 1817) when he was off again, this time to the United States. He left England in March 1818, and in July 1818 exhibited two paintings (now lost) at the Pennsylvania Academy of Fine Arts. These were *Full Length Portrait of a Gentleman* and *Portrait of a Gentleman*. A contemporary description supplied to William Dunlap by a certain Thomas Cummings provides an insight into the artist's activities at that time. 'He when in America exercised his profession in New York, living in the house with Mr. Cummings, the father of the well-known miniature painter. This was in 1818. Thomas S. Cummings, then a boy, was encouraged in his attempts at art by Earl, and possesses many of his sketches which are replete with character. Mr. Cummings describes Earle as being at that time a fair-complexioned, flaxen-haired young man. He is probably now as black as his favorites of the South Sea Islands.'[9] If the brown-haired self-portrait of the artist painted six years later on Tristan da Cunha is any record of Earle's real appearance, then Dunlap's wry conclusions were borne out and the boy Thomas Cummings was mistaken in his recollection of the artist.

Fortunately there is slightly more information describing the artist's 'rambles' in South America. He met the English authoress Maria Graham (afterwards Lady Callcott) in Rio and provided illustrations for her *Journal of a Voyage to Brazil, and Residence There, During Part of the Years 1821, 1822, 1823* (published in 1824).[10] His eagerness to explore the continent resulted in a voyage around the coast of South America, travelling up the west coast to Lima, where he may have witnessed Lord Cochrane's historic blockade of Callao Harbour in November 1820, and then as far as Cape Frio and Pernambuco on the east coast. 'And, towards the commencement of 1824 [actually on 17 February], having received the most flattering offers of introduction to Lord Amherst, who had just left England to take upon himself the government of India, Mr. Earle resolved on quitting Rio, and proceeding to the Cape of Good Hope, thence intending to take his passage to Calcutta. Wearied, however, with awaiting the arrival of a vessel bound to the Cape, he was enterprising enough, contrary to the advice of all his friends at Rio, to intrust himself on board the *Duke of Gloucester*, a worn-out Margate hoy, which was proceeding thither with potatoes, laden to the water's edge.'[11]

Some weeks after leaving Rio de Janeiro fierce storms and squalls forced

8 Earle, *Narrative* (1966), p.50.

9 Dunlap, *Rise and Progress* (1965), v.3, p.107.

10 These illustrations were engraved by Edward Finden after Earle. Copies of Earle's drawings for the plates were made by his brother-in-law, Denis Dighton, and are in the British Museum.

11 Earle, *Narrative* (1966), p.50.

the leaking vessel to heave to by the remote island of Tristan da Cunha. Excited by the thought of spending some time on shore after the cramped quarters and unseasonable weather he had lately experienced, Earle eagerly set off, accompanied by his dog and taking his sketchbook with him. That 'this was a spot hitherto unvisited by any artist' added to the attraction of the island. His restlessness and curiosity proved disastrous. Three days later Earle was preparing to launch the boat which was to take him back to the vessel 'when the sloop tacked, and stood out to sea! I concluded she was only making a long stretch, and waited on the beach some hours; but she stood quite off to sea, and I never beheld her more!'[12]

In his journal, Earle relates the anxiety and loneliness of the next eight months spent as a castaway on the island. He was not, however, entirely alone, as the melancholy tone of some of the journal entries at times suggests. There were six other permanent adult residents on the island. With characteristic resourcefulness, Earle managed to occupy the time organising dangerous hunting expeditions in search of food, painting (until his supply of material ran out), educating the Governor's children and acting as chaplain on Sundays.

Certainly, the changeable weather and sombre geography of the desolate island depressed him enormously. The journal records his sudden changes of mood — one moment deeply affected by the uncertainty and seeming hopelessness of his situation; the next affectionately praising the kindness and generosity of his new friends. 'No sooner does night set in than the air is full of nocturnal birds, whose screams are particularly mournful; and then comes the painful reflection, that I am so many thousands of miles from every human haunt, and separated from all my friends and family, who are in total ignorance of where I am, or what has become of me. But I force myself to struggle against dismal thoughts, unwilling that my comrades (who do every thing in their power to console me) should suspect how much I suffer . . . though we have no wine, grog, or any other strong drink, there is no lack of jovial mirth in any of the company.'[13] This isolation from congenial company, from friends and family, proved to be the greatest hardship for the gregarious artist. Two months later, after being rescued from the island, he wrote that his companions' background and interests were so different from his own that 'they were but little calculated to alleviate the mortification of my situation'.[14]

In another change of mood, Earle extolled the virtues of his abstemious and spartan way of life. 'Exercise and temperance we all believe to be greatly conducive to health. Five months' residence on this island has convinced me of their wonderful effects on the constitution. . . . These last four months' experience has done more to convince me of the "beauty of temperance" than all the books that ever were written could have done. I now begin to think the life of an anchorite was not so miserable as is generally imagined by the gay and dissipated. . . .'[15] Earle's enthusiasm for the 'beauty of temperance' was short-lived; it is likely that in Rio de Janeiro Earle, like many of his fellow Europeans, frequently sought comfort and refreshment in liquor. His spirited descriptions of rowdy carnival celebrations in a Rio brothel have a spontaneity which suggests a first-hand knowledge of the establishment. Later, in New Zealand, Earle incurred the censure and disapproval of the

12 Earle, *Journal* (1966), p.206.
13 Earle, *Journal* (1966), p.221.
14 *Hobart Town Gazette and Van Diemen's Land Advertiser*, 18 February 1825.
15 Earle, *Journal* (1966), p.235-6.

June Park, Van Dieman's Land,
perfect Park Scenery (no. 57; 1825)

Wesleyan missionaries both for his liaisons with native women and for his addiction to the bottle.

On 29 November 1824, the artist's term of confinement ended when a vessel observed his frantic signals and (unlike previously sighted vessels, which had totally ignored the signals) braved the heavy surf that surrounded the island in order to rescue him. 'She proved to be the "Admiral Cockburn", bound for Van Diemen's Land.'[16] After a voyage of some seven weeks the vessel arrived in Hobart, Tasmania, on 18 January 1825.

Earle meticulously recorded the topography around Hobart. His water-colour sketches (now in the Mitchell Library) were later made into a panorama by Robert Burford and exhibited in London in 1831. Presumably the artist lived in New Town, Hobart, for a while, since he wrote to the *Hobart Town Gazette and Van Diemen's Land Advertiser* from that place, in a letter dated 12 February, describing his experiences and adventures as a castaway. He also travelled ninety kilometres northwest of Hobart to paint the verdant pastures of the Bothwell district, recorded in *June Park, Van Dieman's Land, perfect Park Scenery* (no. 57).

Four months later in Hobart, Earle boarded the brig *Cyprus*, arriving in Sydney on 14 May. After the limited society and simple lifestyle of Tristan da Cunha, the gregarious artist must have revelled in the attention, invitations and convivial company he found in Sydney, no doubt abandoning the abstemious existence. He quickly established himself as the first painter in the colony, replacing the less sophisticated portrait and miniature painter Richard Read (senior). Earle was commissioned by the emancipists to decorate the dining room for the farewell banquet in honour of Governor Brisbane. The result was not a resounding success. A reviewer for the *Sydney Gazette*, describing the work in 1829, one year after Earle's departure from Sydney Town, was hardly complimentary. 'Mr. Earle painted . . . a transparency, representing Diogenes with a lanthorn in his hand, searching through "this varsal worlde" for a honest man, and at length finding one in the person of Sir Thomas. The representation was too childish to have been the offspring of Mr. Earle's refined taste, though it may of his sportive fancy . . . Sir Thomas's infant daughter screamed with horror when told that "the honest man" was her father.'[17]

Nevertheless, shortly afterwards the 'favourite artist' was given a second, more important commission. Early in November, the Civil Officers of New South Wales commissioned a full-length oil portrait of Governor Brisbane[18] as 'a monument of the progress of the fine arts in New South Wales under his Excellency's administration'.[19] The Brisbane portrait was followed by two other commissions, the large, grandiose portraits of *Captain John Piper* and *Mrs. John Piper and her Children*, now in the Mitchell Library, Sydney.

Throughout 1826, Earle continued to paint portraits of prominent personages in the colony. He painted Frederick Goulburn,[20] the Colonial Secretary, and a study of Dr Robert Townson (now in the Mitchell Library). Earle's portraits of Mrs Blaxland,[21] James Dunlop, Mrs Underwood and child and Messrs Lawson and Underwood were exhibited in his gallery and are

16 Earle, *Journal* (1966), p.243.
17 *Sydney Gazette*, 28 July 1829.
18 This painting still hangs in Government House, Sydney.
19 The *Australian*, 10 November 1825.
20 Now in Parliament House, Sydney.
21 The portrait of Mrs Blaxland has been attributed to Earle, but McGarvie himself was uncertain that the work was painted by Earle. He wrote in the *Sydney Gazette* of 30 July 1829: 'The picture had been in the East Indies and back, and

described by the Reverend John McGarvie.[22] However, their present where-abouts remain unknown. At the end of 1826 or early in 1827 Earle lived for a while at Denham Court, then the residence of Captain Richard Brooks. As a gesture of thanks for the hospitality he had received there, Earle painted portraits of Captain Brooks and his wife.[23] He also painted portraits of their daughter Christiana Jane Blomfield[24] and her husband Captain Thomas Blomfield.[25] These are all less sophisticated portraits, primarily concerned with giving the patron the standard realistic 'likeness' he was seeking.

In July 1826 Earle advertised the opening of his art gallery at No. 10 George Street, Sydney, which was described by McGarvie in his diary[26] as well as in the *Sydney Gazette*.[27] He also gave lessons and advertised 'a large Assortment of every description of Articles used in Drawing, Painting &c.'[28] which he sold from these premises. In August the 'indefatigable Mr Earle' obtained a lithographic press and began publishing a set of *Views in Australia*. These views were lithographed and hand-coloured by the artist.[29]

The versatility and energy of the artist was obviously well known. In that year also he was engaged to paint illusionistic scenery (classical statues of Apollo and Minerva) around the interior of the makeshift theatre then situated above the old courthouse in Castlereagh Street.

Towards the end of 1826, Earle journeyed inland to sketch the Blue Mountains, Bathurst and the Wellington Valley, and the Hunter River. He then travelled north of Sydney as far as Port Stephens and Port Macquarie. During February 1827 he painted eight views from the top of Palmer's Hill, Sydney, which Burford used for his panorama. They were exhibited at Leicester Square in 1829-30. In April and May the artist penetrated further south to explore and record the sub-tropical Illawarra rainforest. During the ride home he broke his leg and was forced to recuperate at Macquarie Grove, Cowpastures. Earle appreciated the humorous aspects of his plight and wrote a comical description of the accident to a friend in Sydney:

> But now my jokes I must curtail, my own mishap to tell
> 'Twas on the last days journey, the accident befel . . .
> A log of wood lay in the road, my [leg] [i]t did assail
> So violent the shock I felt, crash crack there goes the bone
> O here's a pretty mess I'm in, I wish I was at home.[30]

On 20 October 1827, Earle sailed for New Zealand on board the *Governor Macquarie*, filled with 'hopes of finding something new for my pencil in their peculiar and picturesque style of life'.[31] While not the first artist to visit New Zealand, Earle was the first to take up residence there. He later published

suffered considerably from the heat of an inter-tropical climate . . . . We are not certain whether this picture was painted by Mr. Earle, but it formed a prominent object in his gallery.' However, as all the other works in the exhibition were painted by Earle, it seems unlikely that the portrait of Mrs Blaxland was not.

22 *Sydney Gazette*, 30 July 1829.
23 Australian National Gallery.
24 Location unknown.
25 Private collection.
26 ML 1332, p.235.
27 28 July 1829, 30 July 1829.
28 *Sydney Monitor*, 8 September 1826.
29 They consisted of three views of Sydney entitled: *Sydney Heads, View from the Sydney Hotel* and *H.M.S. Warspite coming to Anchor off Sydney Cove*.
30 *Letter to Mrs Ward*, ML Ae 23.
31 Earle, *Narrative* (1966), p.193.

View from the Summit of Mount York,
N.S. Wales (no. 82; c.1826-7)

A Bullock Hackery or Cow Coach of
India (no. 153; 1829)

an account of the nine months spent in the North Island.[32] One of the most striking features of this narrative is Earle's genuinely warm and friendly attitude towards the Maoris; unlike the missionaries on the island, he did not consider them socially or intellectually inferior 'savages'. Nor did he treat them as heathen children, but accepted the friendship and protection of King George and his tribe and lived with them at the Bay of Islands for some months.

Conscious of the childlike and violent nature of the Maoris, he was convinced that further contact with Western civilisation and improved methods of technology could only have beneficial results. 'All appear eager for improvement, full of energy, and indefatigably industrious, and possessing amongst themselves, several arts which are totally unknown to their neighbours.'[33] Earle was appalled at the New Zealanders' occasional feasts of human flesh and once, at the risk of his life, impetuously attempted to stop such an event from taking place.

He was also wryly amused at the cunning attempts of the New Zealanders to conceal aspects of their lives of which they knew the white men disapproved. Despite appearances to the contrary, they maintained only a superficial respect for the Sabbath. 'It was the custom . . . to refrain from all kinds of work on the Sabbath; . . . and, strange to say, the natives also abstained from working on that day. . . . Not a bit of work would they do upon a Sunday, although it was a critical time with them; for all the chiefs were unprepared with their war canoes for the approaching expedition. At length we discovered that their cunning was as conspicuous as their politeness. They had observed we generally lay longer in bed on a Sunday morning than any other; they accordingly were up by break of day, and had completed many hours' work before we made our appearance; but the moment one of us did appear, the work was instantly left off.'[34]

As a result of his friendship with the whaling captains, some of whom were living with Maori women, Earle incurred the hostility of the Wesleyan missionaries. Their cold and inhospitable behaviour irretrievably biased Earle's attitude towards them and they are vehemently criticised in his narrative, attacks which aroused much controversy when published. Writers for the *Edinburgh Review* and the *Protestant Journal* were among those who censured him.

On 5 May 1828, Earle returned to Sydney. He then determined to proceed to India,[35] and left the coast of Australia in the *Rainbow* on 12 October 1828 to become the first freelance artist to paint in the South Pacific. 'This vessel touched at the Caroline Islands, proceeded to Guam, one of the Ladrones, thence to Manilla, and afterwards to Sincapoor; where he was introduced to "the Resident", who paid him every attention.'[36] Earle's friendly nature, good humour and easy mode of address stood him in good stead during his travels. He mixed easily in different types of society, not only with Her Majesty's representatives in the colonies he visited, but also with the Maoris and whaling captains in New Zealand, or the cheerful, honest seafaring inhabitants of Tristan da Cunha.

32 Augustus Earle, *A Narrative of A Nine Months' Residence in New Zealand in 1827; Together With a Journal of a Residence in Tristan D'Acunha, an Island Situated Between South America and the Cape of Good Hope* (London: Longman, 1832).
33 Earle, *Narrative* (1966), p.187.
34 Earle, *Narrative* (1966), p.129-30.
35 Earle, *Narrative* (1966), p.50-1.
36 Earle, *Narrative* (1966), p.50-1.

'The vessel then sailed through the Straits of Malacca to Pulo-Penang, he enriching his portfolio at every resting-place. At Madras he acquired both fame and money; and during his short stay there executed the original drawings of that Presidency, which have been since copied and exhibited as a Panorama, by Messrs. Daniell and Parris. While in the zenith of his celebrity, his health unfortunately declined, and he was advised to leave India with as little delay as possible; and, feeling convinced his life depended on his speedy departure, he immediately went down to Pondicherry, taking thence his passage to England, . . . on board "La Julie", . . . but being overtaken by adverse gales, the captain was compelled to lighten his vessel by throwing overboard the whole of the cargo, and after considerable difficulty made the Mauritius; . . . During the stay of this vessel at the Mauritius, Mr. Earle executed a series of beautiful panoramic views of this picturesque and interesting island.'[37]

During the voyage back to England the *Resource* (the vessel Earle had boarded in Mauritius) called at St Helena, where he painted *Napoleons Tomb in the Island of St. Helena* (no. 155).

Earle probably arrived back in England late in 1829. He characteristically set about capitalising on his experiences abroad. *Views in New South Wales, and Van Diemen's Land: Australian Scrap Book, 1830*[38] was published in 1830, while *A Narrative of A Nine Months' Residence in New Zealand in 1827; Together With a Journal of a Residence in Tristan D'Acunha, an Island Situated Between South America and the Cape of Good Hope* was published in 1832. Despite his poor health and the hazards he had encountered during his travels abroad, Earle was eager to set off again. He did not have long to wait. 'An opportunity soon offered, and he unhesitatingly availed himself of it; accepting the situation of draughtsman to his Majesty's ship "Beagle", commanded by Captain FitzRoy.'[39] He sailed from Plymouth on 27 December 1831.

The only surviving description of the voyage from Plymouth to Bahia is an engraving in FitzRoy's journal[40] taken from a lively drawing, *Crossing the Line*, in which he noted the boisterous practical joking which traditionally accompanied this ceremony. Two graceful drawings, one of San Salvador, Bahia, and the other of Rio de Janeiro, which they reached on 4 April, are also illustrated in FitzRoy's narrative. Earle shared a cabin with Charles Darwin during the voyage and the two became firm friends. Darwin mentions the artist several times in his diary, adding that they were to share a house at Rio: 'at Botofogo Earl [sic] & myself found a most delightful house which will afford us most excellent lodgings . . . Earl makes an excellent guide, as he formerly lived some years in the neighbourhead [sic].'[41] He took an almost

37 Earle, *Narrative* (1966), p.51.
38 These consisted of two sets of views of Sydney with four plates in each, which were bound together in one volume. Part I consisted of *The North Head of Port Jackson, View of Point Piper, Coming to an anchor off Sydney Cove*, and *Natives of N.S. Wales*, while *Bungaree, Government House, A Government jail gang*, and *Mrs. Macquarie's Seat Government Domain* made up Part II.
39 Earle, *Narrative* (1966), p.51.
40 Robert FitzRoy, *Narrative of the Surveying Voyages of His Majesty's Ships Adventure and Beagle, between the Years 1826 and 1836, Describing Their Examination of the Southern Shores of South America, and the Beagle's Circumnavigation of the Globe*. 3 vols. (London: Henry Colburn, 1839).
41 Charles Darwin, *Diary of the Voyage of H.M.S. Beagle*, ed. Nora Barlow (Cambridge: Cambridge University Press, 1933), p.48.

obsessive interest in Earle's health, noting every symptom in his journal and letters home. Earle, who was suffering from rheumatism, did not accompany the young scientist on his excursions into the surrounding countryside. His poor health forced him to remain on shore for all but two of the *Beagle's* subsequent voyages, which must have been galling to him, accustomed as he was to new sights and activity. Finally, as a result of continuing sickness, he resigned as official draughtsman and was replaced by Conrad Martens. The details concerning Earle's departure from the *Beagle* are confused, as FitzRoy states that Earle did not remain on board after August 1832. However it is known that Earle was on board the *Beagle* when it returned to Montevideo from Bahia Blanca on 26 October 1832. The *Beagle* left four days later for Buenos Aires and returned sometime between 14-26 November 1832, but it is not known if Earle was still on board at this date.

The lack of biographical details concerning the final years of Earle's life suggests a period of loneliness and seclusion brought on by his deteriorating health. He died alone, aged forty-six, on 10 December 1838 at 9 Diana Place, London. His death was attributed to 'asthma and debility'.[42]

Earle and topographical art

Earle's paintings record his travels and observations, and it was natural that he chose to paint in a medium suited to his nomadic existence. Watercolour was both a portable and eminently suitable medium for rapid record.[43] By the beginning of the nineteenth century, a British watercolour school had begun to emerge with the work of such artists as Paul Sandby and Thomas and William Daniell, who adopted Sandby's topographical approach to landscape — an ideal approach for the description of interesting places.

The Daniells may have instructed Earle in the rudiments of painting, after their return from India in 1794, when they resided at Fitzroy Square, where Earle lived after 1809. William Daniell was also acquainted with Earle's sister, Phoebe. A training in the conventions of topographical art would have been useful to Earle, being the form of approach traditionally chosen by travel artists. The Daniells' firmly constructed and clearly defined compositions, and their emphasis on accuracy, may well have influenced Earle's compositions. So might their orderly placement of forms and treatment of figures. The position of the figure in *View near Lower Heysham, Lancashire, March 1, 1816* (in *A Voyage Round Great Britain*), and the whimsical drawing of the figure itself, recall Earle's *View from the Summit of the South Head near Sidney* [sic] (no. 63). Earle's treatment of the Negroes and Portuguese in the Brazilian watercolours recalls William Daniell's expressive portraits of the Boers with natives in *African Scenery and Animals*. The sketchily defined travellers of William Daniell's *The Daniells at Work* remind one of Earle's figures in *Water Fall, Penang* (no. 150). The Daniells' influence would have encouraged and stimulated the young artist's travel plans.

Earle's indebtedness to topographical art is apparent from an examination of the work of artists such as Francis Towne (1739 or 1740-1816), John White Abbott (1763-1851) and William Pars (1742-1782). White Abbott confined his sketching to Scotland and the Lakes District, but Towne and Pars travelled and painted abroad. Their flat, linear compositions, with thinly applied washes of colour bounded by a fine outline, would seem ancestors of some

42 Certified copy of his death certificate, Somerset House, London.
43 Watercolour had become a more suitable medium than oil with the commercial production from 1780 of pans or cakes of watercolour by Thomas and William Reeves.

of Earle's Australian, New Zealand and Indian watercolours.[44] White Abbott's work displays an element of poetry often lacking in topographic art. His *Old Man at Coniston* (1791), a rather graceful study of the Lakes District, has a serene, almost pastoral quality which is close to some of Earle's New Zealand watercolours — particularly *Bay of Islands, New Zealand* (no. 118). His delicate, feathery treatment of foliage also links him with Earle.[45]

It is interesting that Earle showed little stylistic development in the eight or nine years which separate the Brazilian watercolours from those painted in the South Pacific. To a large extent, his situation was responsible. He was painting in remote parts of the world, away from contact with other artists, and could not have kept abreast of contemporary innovations in the medium. In terms of technical accomplishment, then, he must rank behind great water colourists of the day such as Girtin and Turner. His technique relied on the training he received before he left London in 1818, and on his own experiments with the medium. In fact, it is misleading to refer to Earle's stylistic development; it is more accurate to discuss Earle's style in terms of his adaptation to the particular demands of the landscape.

Earle's basic training followed the topographic conventions of eighteenth-century painting; his love of travelling and exploring, and his attitude to nature, however, demonstrate a closer affinity to the nineteenth century.

Earle and the Romantic Movement

An examination of attitudes to nature in the eighteenth century shows the gradual development of theories based on emotional rather than rational principles, culminating in the Romantic Movement: the cult of the individual and the emphasis upon feeling and emotions.

The Picturesque, in emphasising visual qualities at the expense of rational or intellectual qualities, can be interpreted as a prelude to Romanticism. It stands midway between the ordered intellectualism of classical art and the sensual involvement of the Romantics. The development of landscape theories in the eighteenth and early nineteenth centuries reflects this change in attitude. The Romantics believed in the underlying bond between man and nature, holding the pantheistic notion that extensions of man's spirit existed in nature. An individual could only feel 'whole' by co-existing and communing with nature.

Earle's empiricism combined with his attitude to nature in a modified Romantic attitude. He feels at one with nature and wishes to depict the *genius loci*, but is not a victim of nature's crushing forces; nor overwhelmed by its sublimity (both important aspects of the Romantic vision).[46] In Earle's 'Romanticism', scientific accuracy is softened by poetic expression, the two concepts *reinforcing* one another. This attitude is evident in nineteenth-century English landscape painting; in the work of Constable, Girtin, Cotman and Turner, powerful observation and a desire for accurate reportage is not obscured by concern for 'poetic form'. Constable's intimate interpretations of a familiar landscape depend upon the interest in science that led to his own

---

44 *See* nos 67, 107, 139, 153 and 154. These compare favourably with Towne's paintings of Tivoli.

45 *See* White Abbott's *Kerswell, Devon* and Earle's sketch of *Point Piper, New South Wales* (no. 80).

46 On the other hand, man does not feel superior to nature, nor does he possess the picturesque concern to reorder the scene according to aesthetic principles and his own tastes.

observational and environmental studies, allowing him to interpret correctly the atmosphere and light of his surroundings. In the same way, Earle adapted his technique to reproduce the exact light and atmosphere peculiar to a region. This linking of science and self-expression occurs also in the poetry of Wordsworth, who considered that the poet must employ scientific accuracy in his search for truth, emphasising that the poet's primary ability must be 'the ability to observe with accuracy things as they are in themselves and with fidelity to describe them'.[47]

Alongside this 'empiric Romanticism' in Earle's work, there are some elements which would have been considered 'typically' Romantic by his contemporaries. His paintings exhibit Romantic tendencies however only when the subject itself is of a romantic nature, such as the strange and wild scenery he encountered on the south coast of New South Wales, and set down in *View on the Coast of N.S. Wales Ilawarra* (no. 98). McGarvie's description ran thus: 'an ideal view of a huge perforated rock in the foreground, with the sea at a distance. The beauty of this picture depended on the strong light and shade forming a contrast, and seemed as if one were contemplating beautiful scenery from the window of a darkened chamber.'[48] From the dark recesses of the cave we look through the window to the foaming surf which surrounds the isolated, cathedral-like rock structure, reminiscent of an ancient ruin (a favourite Romantic image). Earle contrasts the sombre cavernous 'interior', the tall jagged rock structure and the breaking waves in the centre of the painting with the clear serenity of the sky above, where the birds soar freely. He paints the black solidity of massed forms and the turbulence of the waves, while at the same time evoking the ephemeral: a delicate sea-sprayed atmosphere dusting the far-off headland. Further contrast is provided by the romantic solitary figure standing on the rocky foreshore.

Earle's contemporaries also considered his Tristan da Cunha watercolours highly romantic. McGarvie wrote, 'Mr. Earle's representations also of romantic scenery in Tristan D'Acunha, where he resided nine months with Governor Glass, were much admired here. . . .'[49] He continued, 'These as may be easily supposed are of the most romantic character. The peak splintered summits and huge rocks of the island are well expressed. . . .'[50] By 'romantic', McGarvie means wild and strange, and on Tristan da Cunha, both the situation and the subject matter were extremely romantic. The dramatic landscape and stormy seas are thus depicted in a manner which emphasises the drama of the subject, involving the Cotmanesque superimposing of blocks of colour, and almost expressionistic brushwork with long, curling strokes of *A North Easter, Tristan D'Acunha* (no. 48) and *Rafting Blubber at Tristan D'Acunha* (no. 47). The situation of the castaway and the disaster of the shipwreck were inevitable consequences of the increase in sea traffic in the nineteenth century and demonstrate to the artist nature's indifference to humanity. The image of the shipwreck was an old allegorical device, easily adapted to Romantic sentiment in Gericault's *Raft of the Medusa* (1818-19) and Friedrich's *Shipwreck of the Hope* (1822).[51]

Earle's enforced 'exile' on this isolated land resulted in occasional bouts of melancholia. He wrote: 'Looking out from my abode, no spot in the world

47 William Wordsworth, *Poems* (London, 1815), p.viii.
48 *Sydney Gazette*, 30 July 1829.
49 *Sydney Gazette*, 28 July 1829.
50 *Sydney Gazette*, 30 July 1829.
51 *See also* L. Eitner, 'The open window and the storm-tossed boat: an essay in the iconography of Romanticism', *Art Bulletin* 37 (1953):281-90.

Solitude, — Tristan D'Acunha, —
Watching the horizon (no. 39; 1824)

can be more desolate; particularly on a blowing night.'[52] Solitude is necessary to the Romantic state, permitting the meditation, introspection and self-analysis indulged in by Romantic poets, who frequently expressed their personal misery and suffering. It was a subject which appealed greatly during the first two decades of the nineteenth century to painters such as Friedrich, Fuseli and Joseph Wright of Derby.

Earle's desolation and frustration are reflected in the watercolour entitled *Solitude, — Tristan D'Acunha, — Watching the horizon* (no. 39), in which he painted himself alone with his dog on a rocky headland, overlooking a panorama of raging surf, and despondently gazing out to sea. 'I station myself upon the rocks, straining my eyes with looking along the horizon in search of a sail, often fancying the form of one where nothing is, . . . and again I retire to my lodging with increased melancholy and disappointment!'[53] The Romantic emotion which dominates Earle's descriptions of his experience on Tristan da Cunha is that which permeates Tennyson's later romantic poem, *Enoch Arden* (published in 1864). Enoch recounts his loneliness and desperation as a shipwrecked sailor:

> . . . or all day long
> Sat often in the seaward-gazing gorge,
> A shipwrecked sailor, waiting for a sail:
> No sail from day to day . . .

In both Romantic literature and painting, then, 'castaway' subject matter and expressions of gloom and solitude such as Earle's were popular themes. The mood of despondency in the painting is further intensified by the sombre charcoal colouring, and the lighter greys indicating the mist and spray. Such depression is however exceptional in Earle's work. It was only when thrust into a situation over which he had no control that this Romantic melancholy took hold of him.

Australian art also reveals a strong element of Romanticism in one of its themes: the noble frontiersman. The basic characteristics of the noble frontiersman are those of the noble savage: 'Both were guileless, yet not gullible, sons of "nature" . . . .'[54] The first signs of this attitude towards the frontiersman occurred in the early 1820s, as a result of the colonial expansion in New South Wales after the recall of Governor Macquarie. It was only then that people began to realise more fully the great diversity of the Australian scenery in these newly discovered areas — the sub-tropical Illawarra district, Port Stephens, and the Bathurst plains, to name but a few. Settlers began to exploit new areas for grazing purposes. Contemporary travel accounts stressed the challenges and freedoms of frontier life. In *Settlers and Convicts: or Recollections of Sixteen Years' Labour in the Australian Backwoods*, Alexander Harris gives a contemporary account of cattle-raising in the Australian backwoods, writing of the dangers encountered in the bush; the hardships and the loneliness; but describing also the hardworking, resourceful nature of the frontiersmen. He was particularly impressed by their friendliness, good humour and generosity. Although Australia as a recent settlement was cut off from one of the major sources of Romantic feeling — the cult of the past — there were three important sources of Romantic sentiment to be found in the colony: an admiration for a free and adventurous outdoor life; the Romantic desire to escape from the real world and to live close to nature; and the Romantic delight in exploring unknown, 'virgin' country.

52 Earle, *Journal* (1966), p.221.
53 Earle, *Journal* (1966), p.227.
54 Russel Ward, *The Australian Legend* (Melbourne: Oxford University Press, 1958), p.230.

The concept of the noble frontiersman helped to make popular the practice of 'bivouacking', or camping in the open air. Until 1820 there had been no need for travellers to camp en route to their destination, as areas of settlement were still fairly confined and the distance between them could be easily covered in a day. Needless to say, bivouacking and sleeping on the ground under the stars gratified the Romantic yearning to be at one with nature.

Earle painted both frontier life and bivouacking scenes, with the exotic, lush vegetation of the Illawarra a fitting setting.[55] Generally these paintings are naturalistic in character, showing the settlers bivouacking (as in *A Bivouack, day break, on the Ilawarra Mountains*, no. 95) and travelling (*Cabbage Tree Forest, Illawarra, New South Wales*, nos 93-4). In both the watercolour study and oil painting for the work entitled *A Bivouac [sic] of Travellers in Australia, in a Cabbage-tree Forest, day break* (no. 3), Earle exploited the dramatic and romantic potential of the subject matter. The faint light of dawn illuminates only the group in the foreground, silhouetted against a sombre backdrop of cedar trees, foliage and cobalt sky, shot with the orange-pink and pale-blue flickering light of dawn. The cabbage trees, with their fern-like fronds visible against the pale morning light, contribute to the exotic atmosphere of the painting. Attention is focused upon the foreground, where frontiersmen, travellers and native guides are seen preparing for the day ahead.

The massive cedar trunks provide a striking setting for the action in *A Bivouack, day break, on the Ilawarra Mountains* (no. 96). Two slanting trees in the foreground provide a compact framework through which the action is viewed — that is, in the centrally 'lit' area. The figures by the hollow tree appear to be hiding or taking refuge in the tree, raising the possibility that the painting was intended as a companion piece to *Skirmish, Bush Rangers & Constables, Ilawarra* (no. 100) and that the men in the middleground are escaped convicts. The drama of the scene is intensified by the high viewpoint, so that we seem to be looking down on the painting. A similar device is used in *Cabbage Tree Forest, Ilawarra, New South Wales* (no. 93), where the massive trees, often only partially evident, and abundant vegetation dwarf the tiny human figures, enhancing the Romantic notion of man being overwhelmed by nature. The efforts of the frontiersmen to forge a living for themselves by taming this wilderness thus seem the more heroic.

The Illawarra is again the setting for the study of bushrangers and constables in no. 100, mentioned above. Alexander Harris later explained that convicts occasionally escaped from bondage and lived by stealing cattle and thieving from the settlers until apprehended by the constables. This painting is a graphic description of the resulting 'skirmish'. In the foreground a bag of loot lies open, revealing jewellery and other stolen goods. Movement, action and expression are vigorously delineated. The composition is unusual; the action stretches diagonally across the painting, from the fore- to the middleground, in a zigzag of tension. Only the lower halves of the trees, surrounded by thick dark undergrowth, are evident, limiting the area within which the action takes place and serving to intensify the dramatic impact of the scene.

A slightly different conception of the noble frontiersman is expressed in *The Blue Mountains from the Emu Plains' road* (no. 92). This clear, sunny watercolour is set in the fertile greenness of the Bathurst ranges. Earle has placed the traveller-frontiersman on the crest of a hill, overlooking a panorama of mountains, valleys and luminescent sky. One feels a strong auto-

55 Such as nos 94-6 and 99-100.

A Bivouack, day break, on the
Illawarra Mountains (no. 95; 1827)

biographical element in the painting; Earle seems to identify with the free, untrammelled existence and hardy optimism of the prospective young settler. The traces of dawn and iridescent new light which flood the watercolour add to this impression of hope, adventure and opportunity. The painting is essentially a lucid description of the subject, combined with a Romantic reference to the noble frontiersman.

In these Illawarra paintings, Earle generally uses both indirect and direct methods to enhance the Romantic aspects of the paintings. Allusions to the noble frontiersman, to the practice of bivouacking and to pioneering exploration are combined with technical effects, such as the direct use of contrasts in lighting, elevated viewpoints and striking compositional arrangements, to highlight the dramatic overtones of the subject matter.

Earle's relation of style to place

There is considerable variety in the way Earle handled the different groups of watercolours he painted in remote parts of the world. The little-known South American and South Pacific landscapes are among his most technically accomplished. Colour, light and atmosphere are rendered by the use of subdued washes, while minute brushstrokes delineate individual details with exquisite care. The broader dabs of paint which appear in some of the less competent Australian and New Zealand works are absent. In the Tristan da Cunha watercolours, Earle also demonstrates his superb sense of colour, shape and design. The Australian paintings are possibly the most unusual, owing to the great diversity within the group, in both technique and accomplishment. This two-fold variety is evident from a comparison of two of the works. *The Coast of New Holland, New South Wales* (no. 58) is treated rather awkwardly, and the outline of the coast is heavy-handed. A far more sensitive approach to form and atmosphere occurs in *South Head & Light House. Port Jackson N.S. Wales* (no. 59). The delicate washes of rose, yellow and mauve in the sky are distinguished from the darker tones and long horizontal brushstrokes describing the varying texture of the rocky outcrop and the shadows on the rippling water. Further variations in treatment occur in *On The Hunter River, N.S. Wales* (no. 67) and *Annual Meeting of Native Tribes at Paramatta* (no. 76), discussed below.

Earle's watercolour techniques involved laying in the subject with a pencil, or sometimes a fine pen, and then painting over a neutral ground-wash of local colour; in accordance with general watercolour practice, he worked from light to dark. Usually, green and blue washes predominate for the middle distance. Finally, he employed charcoal, browns or grey-browns, to paint in the darker foreground details, generally rocks and earth.

Earle altered his technique to suit the individual demands of each new place, and an understanding of his watercolour practice is best gained from a chronological examination of each group of paintings.

South America

The South American landscapes combine fine brushstrokes with delicate washes, gradually increasing in intensity, to describe the scenery in an exquisitely lyrical manner. The obvious pleasure the artist found in exploring the lovely scenery around Rio is recorded in no. 15, *From the Summit of the Cacavada Mountains, nr. Rio.* This shows the artist throwing up his hands in delight at the view of the Sugar Loaf and the Corcovado. In these views, Earle has suggested the vaporous mauve-blue haze which continually veils the mountains, together with the clear, sunny weather of Brazil lighting the

From the Summit of the Cacavada
[Corcovado] Mountains, nr. Rio (no. 15;
1821-4)

forms in the foreground. Soft washes of blue-grey tones render the outlines of the background mountains indeterminate. The overall bluish wash links the purple greyness of the distant forms with the pale blue bay in the foreground and the closer objects, seen through a clearer, silvery light, to form a unified composition.[56] The overall impression is of a tranquil, uninterrupted view. In these watercolours (nos 15-17) and in the study of the Laranjeiras further inland (*View near Rio de Janeiro*, no. 18), Earle communicates his own rapport with the scenery. He suggests the restorative powers of this serene and idyllic mountain setting to a spirit exhausted by the hectic lifestyle and cruelty portrayed in the city watercolours. These paintings contrast with the vigorous activity and bright colours of *Negro Fandango Scene, Campo St. Anna nr. Rio* (no. 20) or the stark intensity of the monochrome flagellation scene in *Punishing Negroes at Cathabouco, Rio de Janeiro* (no. 22).

Tristan da Cunha

From the South American scenes we move to the violent storms and sharply contrasted scenery of grey Tristan da Cunha. In 1824 the soothing, calmly beautiful Rio scenery was replaced by a sombre and friendless landscape. The thundering surf, violent squalls and precipitous black mountains could not be described in the same way as Rio de Janeiro, with delicate washes and minute brushstrokes. The artist had to experiment to find a method of expressing the dramatic intensity of his new surroundings.

Some of the watercolours recall Cotman in their broad simplification of mass, and the allocation of areas into flat blocks of colour which form effective patterns, as well as a means of balancing and unifying the composition. Cotman's well-known *Greta Bridge* (in the British Museum) had been exhibited at the Academy in 1806, the same year as Earle's first showing there; he may have been familiar with Cotman's work. Possibly, this familiarity led Earle to experiment further; he juxtaposes shapes in a near-abstract fashion to create striking, essentially two-dimensional designs with little regard for depth. It is the interaction between these shapes which is important — the tension between the different masses and planes of colour, which contrast and complement one another. Earle displays an almost geometric interest in the relationship between these solids and planes. The artist's own emotional reaction to the landscape is also responsible for these forceful designs. As a castaway prisoner, his reaction to the sombre, precipitous landscape and inclement weather was more hostile than it might have been in more favourable circumstances.

At times it seems that the elements are ranked against him, conspiring to prevent his release. In no. 48, *A North Easter, Tristan D'Acunha*, one can sense the gale force pushing against the artist, obstructing him as he struggles to walk along the beach. The waves pounding on to the sand and, beyond, the anthropomorphic cliffs looming in the background, reinforce this threatening image. Earle also accurately describes the characteristic black lava rock formations of the island,[57] repeating the description in his journal. 'All the rocks on the island are of the same dismal hue, which gives a most melancholy aspect to all its scenery.'[58] His attitude to the scenery is evident in no. 47, *Rafting Blubber at Tristan D'Acunha*. In this highly charged expres-

56 In a similar fashion, the atmospheric smoky blue-green 'veil' over *View of the City of Lima . . .* (no. 11) links the shadowy forms of the Andes in the distance with the sea in the foreground. In this subtle painting the pale, superimposed washes describing the mountains beyond are a harmony of fine tonal variations.
57 *See* nos 45, 47, 48 and 52.
58 Earle, *Journal* (1966), p.220.

sionistic seascape, the sky and sea become dense sculptured objects which, with the massive rocks, seem to close in like prison walls upon the figures. Like no. 45, this painting is two-dimensional in character. It is a compact arrangement of hard-edged autonomous shapes, recalling the flats of a stage set; the huge rock on the right is like a solid curtain drawn aside to reveal the *tableau vivant*. The arrangement of forms in no. 44, *Tristan D'Acunha* has similar 'stage-set' qualities in the two-dimensional juxtaposition of rock forms. The outline of the three rock surfaces runs diagonally across the painting to converge at the centre, creating a taut and original composition.

The flatter patchwork arrangement of colour in nos 49 and 50, which depict the view from the summit of Tristan da Cunha and the albatross hunt, are near-abstract designs. These watercolours successfully evoke the contrasts encountered in a rather awesome part of the island to which Earle refers in his journal: 'The sterile and cindery peak, with its venerable head, partly capped with clouds, partly revealing great patches of red cinders, or lava, intermingled with the black rock, produced a most extraordinary and dismal effect. It seemed as though it were still actually burning, to heighten the sublimity of the scene.'[59]

Australia

In most of the Australian watercolours, Earle discards these sombre opaque tones for more transparent washes, brighter colours and a broader, lighter type of brushwork suited to the lighter, sunnier and clearer weather of Australia. The different types of scenery depicted in Australia mean a wider range of colours used; in the smaller groups of watercolours describing other countries, the colours are usually more uniform. The Australian colours range from the sombre, smoky shades of the Illawarra paintings to the clearer, lighter colours of the Blue Mountains and Bathurst plains group, exemplified by the bright greens and yellowy shades of *The Blue Mountains from the Emu Plains' road* (no. 92). The characteristic bluish-grey of the mountains inland from Sydney to the smoky-blue light, less intense than that of the Illawarra, is recorded several times; for example, in no. 85. The final group, in which the colours are different again, consists of the paler pinks, blues and greens in such works as *Female Orphan School, Paramatta N.S. Wales* (no. 68) and *Mr. Cowells Farm on the Coast 60 miles South of Sidney* (no. 97), where soft brushstrokes and delicate washes describe colours and forms muted by a light atmospheric haze.

Occasionally, in order to depict more exactly, darker and more unusual geological forms, Earle calls upon design techniques formulated earlier at Tristan da Cunha. In the watercolours of *Mosmans Cave, Wellington Valley, N.S. Wales* (nos 87-9), he concentrates upon describing the peculiar and unusual limestone formations. Long, curving brushstrokes trace the irregular sculptural shapes in no. 89, a two-dimensional abstract pattern of greys and blacks. The flat patterns of the jagged cave formations of no. 88 are described in similar fashion.

Earle was obviously fascinated by intricate and unusual rock formations. In two other paintings he exploits the design potentials of these surfaces. The contorted shape of the foreground rock in *Curious Rocks & Natural Baths N.S. Wales* (no. 101) seems to be 'answering' the curious prehistoric formation in the middle distance. The eerie atmosphere of these unnatural formations is enhanced by the sombre stillness of the drab grey sea and sky. In the more delicately balanced composition *View on the Coast of N.S. Wales*

59 Earle, *Journal* (1966), p.223.

A man killing Albatross, Tristan
D'Acunha (no. 50; 1824)

Ilawarra (no. 98), Earle's interest in design is again evident, in this case, in the decorative effect gained from looking through the cave 'window' to the weird jagged structure and seascape beyond.

In his desire to present the true character of the Australian landscape, Earle frequently employed broken brushwork — an approach admirably suited to the open nature of the Australian foliage — in *Kings Table Land, Blue Mountains, N.S. Wales* (no. 84) and *Port Jackson, New South Wales* (no. 61). Previous artists had failed to capture this quality, indigenous to the Australian bush; Lycett, for example, tended to paint picturesque, generalised European trees with opaque foliage. Earle, like such nineteenth-century English painters as Constable, recognised that objects become blurred as they recede into the distance, and formulated his technique as a result of his observations, using flecks of paint to suggest forms in the distance. Older artists such as Glover made no allowance for this fact, and tended to paint, in the fore- and middle-ground at least, with the same meticulous clarity.

Earle combined this technique with an overall attempt to convey atmosphere, and its effect on natural phenomena and other forms. In the Illawarra watercolours, the distant figures are accorded this spontaneous, 'impressionistic' handling. The tiny, insubstantial figures dwarfed by the tall cabbage trees and enveloping growth convey some impression of the vast scale, and play an important role in the delineation of depth. Forms, affected by light and atmosphere, become increasingly vague as they recede into depth, and Earle has used minute brushstrokes in the foreground, while lighter dabs of modulated colour, together with muted overall washes, are employed in the middle distance and background, to evoke the misty and humid atmosphere of this sub-tropical region. On Tristan da Cunha, by contrast, depth was achieved through a stage-like recession of planes.

In these paintings, Earle's interest in the effects of atmosphere on form is accompanied by an increasing concern for refined tonalities, and a decrease in precise outlines. The high viewpoint of these Illawarra works (we look down on the scene) and their strong vertical emphasis form a naturalistic treatment of the exuberant growth of a particular type of vegetation, quite inappropriate to the confined pastures of England. In setting down only a section of the landscape, Earle does not permit us to see a framed, picturesque 'view' of the complete scene. Instead, he describes only what he can see — the base of the trees and the dense undergrowth, plunging the observer into the very heart of the forest.

Earle's technical training at the Academy is evident in the devices used to achieve balance and unity, such as the 'staffage' type of tree placement in *Skirmish, Bush Rangers & Constables, Ilawarra* (no. 100). In *A Female Penitentiary, Paramatta N.S. Wales* (no. 71), the trees frame and bind the composition; a topographical treatment divides the simple composition clearly into fore-, middle- and background, with the figures in the middleground placed in such a way that they accentuate the illusion.

Generally, Earle employs more traditional conventions when the landscape is more familiar and reminiscent of 'home'. He shows the ordered definition of the picturesque garden at *Government House & part of the Town of Sidney* (no. 142), designed by Mrs Macquarie, while the pastoral Englishness of the 'perfect Park Scenery' (as Earle himself described it) in *June Park, Van Dieman's Land, perfect Park Scenery* (no. 57) is reminiscent of Paul Sandby, with its emphasis on the graceful tree and shepherd-like figures placed in the centre foreground, with a rustic cottage situated beyond.

Although Earle utilised Academy methods to solve these technical problems, he also formulated his own methods, based on empirical observation, particularly to record atmospheric and meteorological effects. In the Tristan da Cunha watercolours (*see Squall, off Tristan D'Acunha*, no. 40), the changes in weather and the effect they have on land and sea are rendered in a striking and accomplished manner. Earle frequently scratched the surface of the watercolour so that the paper underneath was visible in the form of fine white lines; in nos 141 and 17, these faint glimmers of white denote the play of light on the waves, while in no. 47 they accentuate the foaming surf. Thus the artist found an appropriate idiom to describe particular effects.

Naturalistic observations of meteorological data occur also in the Australian watercolours, particularly in the coastal scenes, where one may occasionally 'read' the weather (*see* no. 62). Storm conditions at sea are studied in *South Head & Light House. Port Jackson N.S. Wales* (no. 59). Such annotations are reminiscent of Constable, as is Earle's interest in meteorological effects, their changing nature and the depiction of squalls and overcast weather.

Earle's sojourn on Tristan da Cunha and his extensive travels by sea afforded him an unlimited opportunity to record maritime scenes. His most effective renderings of the sea are marked by a subtle overlay of tone upon tone; stratified washes which create a translucent rippling surface (as in no. 62, mentioned above),[60] quite similar to Cotman's dextrous wash treatment of the sea in *A Dismasted Brig* (c. 1823).

New Zealand

Earle's watercolours of New Zealand fall into three groups. First, there are the magnificent Romantic studies of the Bay of Islands, in which he has realistically set down the topography of the region, simultaneously charging it with his own delighted response to a beautiful and romantic setting. In his journal the artist enthusiastically described his visit to *Tepoanah, Bay of Islands, Missionary Establishment* (no. 112); 'and it was finally settled that we should cross the bay to Tipoona, a beautiful and romantic spot . . . it was a most delightful trip, the scenery being strikingly beautiful. . . . As the boats approached this lovely spot, I was in an ecstasy of delight.'[61] These larger watercolours are firmly constructed. Brown rocks structure the foreground, which looks over a panoramic stretch of water and fertile valleys, with undulating hills and impressive volcanic mountains rising behind. Charcoal brown predominates, with overall washes of deep greens and blues. The warmth and richness of these colours is accentuated by the pervasive golden light which contributes also to the Romantic mood. While there is no doubt that these paintings have darkened with age, it is also likely that Earle painted them towards the end of the day, when he was able to observe the scenery and inhabitants at leisure. The presence of colour notes[62] suggests that the light faded before he had a chance to complete the paintings.

The next group of New Zealand paintings (nos 109-11, 115-17, 119, 122-3) comprises studies of figures in landscape. The colouring is sombre, owing to a widespread use of brown, dark greens and blues with a heavy, brown-grey foreground. Again it seems that the artist painted late in the day, when the New Zealanders had finished work; they are mostly portrayed standing, or crouched outside their houses. The careful modulations in colour and tone, rich colouring and mellow tints of the Bay of Islands paintings are rarely evident here. Generally, the execution is less competent; for instance,

60 *See also* nos 46, 138 and 141.
61 Earle, *Narrative* (1966), p.140-1.
62 *See* Notes for no. 112.

the background (wash) mountain is awkwardly handled in no. 110 and there is less subtle treatment of rocks and mountain forms in no. 111. However, in the studies of Paroa Bay (no. 116), accuracy is combined with a sensitive pleasure in the beauty of the scene. The problem of fully describing the immense sprawling *pohutukawa* tree without compromising the rest of the picture is successfully resolved, and Earle's preoccupation with unusual phenomena indigenous to foreign places is again evident. In no. 116 he analyses every detail of the tree with the same exactitude that Constable employed in *Bole of an Elm Tree*.[63] The innumerable variations in tone occurring in the limited colour range of smoky browns and greens have been recorded; Earle describes the play of light and shade upon the trunks, foliage and twisting branches of the tree. In both paintings, the background bay and mountains receive equal attention. Delicate grey washes lightly applied suggest the outlines of the hills beyond. The impressionistic rendering of the foreground figures is strikingly effective. The authentic and immediate quality of this competently executed scene would indicate that it was painted on the spot at Paroa Bay.

The paintings in the third group (comprising nos 105, 107-8, 118, 139) are generally lighter in feeling, owing to the absence of heavier, more sombre colours and the use of brighter greens, blues and yellows with pale blue and aqua washes. In addition, Earle left exposed sections of the white paper underneath. In nos 107 and 139 (the illustrations of the Deptford Dockyard), a fine pen line circumscribes flat washes of soft colour (pale blues and greens), so that in no. 107 the pale moss-green foreground is linked to the blues and greens of the bay and hills beyond by a fluid modulation of colour. These delicately balanced works parallel the sophistication and subtle handling of tonal variations in *On The Hunter River, N.S. Wales* (no. 67). In *Entrance of the Bay of Islands New Zealand* (no. 108), Earle adopts a different, highly innovatory form of design. The rather flat, near-abstract patchwork of hills is seen through the tall trees in the extreme foreground. These thin trees form an effective contrast, breaking up the horizontal stretches of flat colour, while the unusual viewpoint contributes to the interest and originality of the painting. As in nos 107 and 139, the subtle colour harmonies within a restricted range from smoky-green to smoky-blue and aqua create a unified composition. The clarity and verisimilitude of these works again suggests on-site portrayal.[64]

The range of approach in the treatment of this third group of New Zealand watercolours demonstrates Earle's versatility in technique. Once again, he has altered his approach to meet the individual demands of the subject matter. At times, as in no. 108, he formulates interesting and unusual designs. He also adjusts his range of colours to accord with the variable times and conditions during which each watercolour was painted.

Guam
Earle recorded his visit to Guam late in 1828 in two watercolours (nos 143 and 144) of Umatac Harbour. In this short period he was able to capture not only the physical characteristics of the island, but the very essence of the region — not just the concrete, but the intangible. He accurately set down physical aspects of the island such as the Spanish Governor's residence, and imbued the works with the somnolent atmosphere and easy

---

63 Victoria and Albert Museum.
64 The fourth group (figure and genre studies) is discussed under the heading 'Earle's portrayal of people'.

lifestyle of the tropics evident in the rendering of the palm trees gently swaying in the breeze. Further back, their thin trunks are whitened by a vertical sliver of light. The naked youths playing on the beach (no. 143) and the natives fishing in the tranquil waters of the bay (no. 144) further contribute to this lazy atmosphere. In no. 144, the calm, pond-like water is effectively conveyed by long, even brushstrokes of neutral washes merging into deep blue, and everything is bathed in a silvery blue light.

Umatak Harbour, Island of Guam, one of the Ladrones (no. 143) is a broad view of the harbour, in which fresh green and pale blues predominate. The mauve haze in the sky suggests a mid- to late-afternoon portrayal, while the background mountain range demonstrates Earle's interest in flatter arrangements of complementary colours. *Umatak, Island of Guam* (no. 144) is a more impressive study, painted from the opposite side of the harbour. A more compact construction defines this 'closer' view of a limited area. There is a finer attention to detail in the delineation of the palm trees and buildings in the middle distance. The fading light intensifies the colours; smoky blues and deep greens predominate, while the majestic grandeur of the background mountains is enhanced by the presence of dark, blue-grey shadows which curve up their sides to form a sculptural pattern of colour.

Malacca and Penang

Earle's watercolours of Malacca are of an extremely high standard, realistically presenting the external features of Malacca and conveying as well his own experience of the town. The grand facades of the Dutch colonial buildings on the right in *Malacca* (no. 146) are meticulously delineated. No less care has been accorded the tilting native houses clustered together on the opposite side of the stream (pictured also in no. 147), or the stick-like palm trees massed together in the left background. In no. 147 (also entitled *Malacca*), the foreground is adroitly linked to the rest of the town by an ancient-looking wooden bridge. The image of what is still today a sleepy little tropical town has been created in such a skilful manner that one feels the urge to cross the bridge and explore it. The details in each case are accorded an 'impressionistic', broken brushwork treatment; the natives and the precious sacred cows in the foreground of no. 147 are also strikingly authentic images of village life. A pervading silver haze recalls the humidity of the day and modifies the colours so that in this painting the houses seem veiled in grey. Cream and flesh-coloured tints in the sky (to the left of the painting) indicate the beginning of a glorious sunset which is lyrically developed in no. 146. The mauve and orange-gold of the dying sun is reflected in the more intense colours of this painting.

Distant View of Malacca (no. 148) is perhaps the most poetic and subtle evocation of a coastal view at sunset found in Earle's *oeuvre*. The painting is a glowing harmony of colours, merging from deep turquoise and blues to the foreground bay and the pale-blue sky shot with cream, gold, crimson and mauve-pink tonalities. Long horizontal brushstrokes describe the gentle lapping of the waves, which complement the soft washes of the sky and vague mountains in the background, rendered obscure by the bluish veil-like mists that succeed the sunset. Tiny brushstrokes define the palm trees and buildings along the shore. Earle records in sunsets the changing quality of muted light and its effect on forms in landscape, particularly when viewed over a coastal panorama (see also *Port Jackson, New South Wales*, no. 60).

Malacca (no. 146; 1828)

In *Water Fall, Penang* (no. 150) the problems encountered in the waterfall study at Waimate, New Zealand (no. 119) have been successfully resolved. At Waimate, he had difficulty in describing the sheer verticality of the landscape, combined with a convincing impression of depth. Both qualities have been convincingly rendered at Penang. Earle also conveys the natural density of the jungle region, emphasised by an encompassing smoky haze in which greys and smoky-greens predominate.

Madras

Earle's next port of call was Madras, where he painted flat, planar designs of intersecting colour. This interest in 'patchwork' effects is evident in some of the Tristan da Cunha, New Zealand and Guam watercolours described earlier (*see* nos 50, 108 and 143). The shapes are generally finely outlined in ink, a practice repeated in other works (nos 67 and 139) and recalling the work of some of the topographic artists described earlier.[65]

Earle described the exotic wares and vibrant colours associated with India, frequently using bright blues and an unusually generous application of vermilion. Both the designs and the fine outlining of forms recall Indian painting. A further note of authenticity is provided by the evocation of sub-tropical humidity in the description of the thick, purple-blue 'blanket' background of nos 153 and 154. Here Earle has once again formulated his own methods to describe the intrinsic character and atmosphere of a region.

Ireland

The later watercolours of Ireland, painted some time between 1834 and 1838, are quite different from the Indian watercolours. The technique Earle employs in *Dunluce Castle County of Antrim, Ireland* (no. 157) is similar, rather, to the solid modelling of some of the Tristan da Cunha examples, in particular no. 47. The artist is preoccupied with a physical analysis of the different structures: mountain, sea and rock. In this painting the eye is led in a wandering pattern to trace the undulating curve of the hills and the looping bridge, combined with a Cezannesque juxtaposing of dense, sculptural forms to create a forceful, tactile, two-dimensional composition.

In no. 158, *(Cape Tennets) Castle Dawson, Derry, Ireland*, the typical accoutrements of a small provincial town are noted: pigs, geese and an ox-drawn cart are disposed in the foreground. The slow pace of life is evident from the relaxed, idle stance of the inhabitants and the lack of traffic in the street. An overall impression of rustic simplicity is conveyed by the straightforward composition and topographic clarity with which the homely little dwellings are rendered.

These watercolours define the true object of the travel artist: to depict not only the physical aspects of each place but also to communicate his personal experience of it in order to make it seem more real to the viewer at home. This Earle did, formulating his own techniques and experimenting with his medium. He sought to describe widely varied regions in Australia, Brazil and the South Pacific, and to depict the effects of weather and climate upon different phenomena. By the use of striking compositional devices he conveyed also a vivid impression of the dramatic land formations he came across in such places as Tristan da Cunha.

Earle's portrayal of people

Earle occasionally adopts a rather brief method of treating people, noting

---

65 Such as Francis Towne's *Elter Force* in the National Gallery of Victoria.

down the outlines with two or three rapid strokes of the brush. He seems more at home with this approach than with more detailed delineations such as the 'close-up' views of the inhabitants in the Tristan da Cunha and some of the Australian scenes, which are more laboured and awkwardly posed. In *View from the Summit of Mount York, N.S. Wales* (no. 82), the articulation of the individual limbs, for example, is particularly weak.

However, it is obvious from a study of the Brazilian watercolours that Earle was capable of accomplished figure studies. He has left us striking portraits of the English, Portuguese and Negro inhabitants of Brazil. *Rita a Celebrated Black Beauty at Rio de Janeiro* (no. 23) leans provocatively against a stone parapet, her taut body and chocolate skin smoothly and skilfully modelled. This glamorous painting contrasts with the stark impact of another Negro study (no. 27), where a youth is sprawled face-down diagonally across the ground, the high viewpoint accentuating the drama of the painting. Both paintings contrast with the pale and emaciated *An Eccliastic of Rio de Janeiro* (no. 24), or the rubicund, fleshy visage of the Empress's rotund equestrian instructor (no. 29), demonstrating Earle's flair for astute characterisation over a wide range of subjects.

Earle's studies of Aborigines vary greatly in standard. In *Wellington Valley, N.S. Wales* (no. 83) and *Mosmans Cave, Wellington Valley, N.S. Wales No. 1* (no. 87) the execution is awkward and anatomically unconvincing. The bodies are squat and have a puppetlike quality. There are of course exceptions. *A Native Family of N.S. Wales* (no. 90) is a truthful appraisal of the expression, poses and anatomy of a 'squatting' Aboriginal family. Earle has convincingly portrayed their awkward, hunched positions, lethargic postures and dull expressions. In *A Native Woman, Australia* (no. 75), a few vigorous lines have produced a forceful study of a scrawny, ageing gin, her face devoid of life. She twists round to face the painter, setting up an effective 'contraposto'. The parts of her body, although viewed from a more complex 'half angle', have been successfully balanced by the artist.

It is worthwhile examining the sketches of Aborigines more closely in order to appreciate their realistic and empirical basis. Earle painted the subjects as they appeared to him at the time; a degraded race heading towards extinction. 'The natives,' he wrote, '. . . seem of the lowest grade. . . . Their limbs are long, thin, and flat, with large bony knees and elbows; a projecting forehead, and pot-belly . . . they have neither energy, enterprise, nor industry. . . . A few exceptions may be met with; but these are the general characteristics.'[66] These 'unhappy beings' are pictured squatting in their humpies or around a campfire (*A Native Camp of Australian Savages* (no. 66), *Mosmans Cave, Wellington Valley, N.S. Wales No. 1* (no. 87) and *A Native Man, Australia* (no. 74)), or on someone else's garden as in *A Native Family of N.S. Wales* (no. 90). Earle conveys the simple nature of these people; they gaze vacantly at us. Even in the tender, lyrical portrait of an attractive young girl (*A Woman of New South Wales*, no. 70) the artist does not attempt to hide the Aborigines' plight. *A Native Woman, Australia* (no. 75) is a truly dejected figure, huddled on the ground with only an old blanket for covering, intent on her own troubles.

Earle understood, perhaps more sympathetically than has been hitherto indicated, the devastating effects of white settlement. Governor Macquarie had instituted annual meetings in order to civilise, educate and assist the Aborigines. However, the original benevolent intention behind these meet-

66 Earle, *Narrative* (1966), p.187.

A Sleeping Negro Brazils — No. 1
(no. 27; 1821-4)

ings had disappeared by the time Earle came to paint them in *Annual Meeting of Native Tribes at Paramatta* (no. 76). The natives are shown receiving handouts of bread and liquor from the soldiers. Crouched like animals on the dirt, mostly naked or scantily clothed, they have been allocated a special area roped off from the white spectators, who watch them from the other side of the enclosure. Earle has both grasped and tried to understand the hopelessness of their situation. He adopts a technique which is somewhere between his more detailed treatment of 'close-up' figures and his sketch-like handling of distant forms. Spontaneous, brief brushstrokes and short, staccato lines combine to present a vivid and effective shorthand account of the event, similar to the work of Rowlandson.

Paintings such as *Desmond, A New South Wales Chief* (no. 77) make it evident however that Earle was aware of the lingering dignity of some Aborigines. Desmond, in his native dress and painted for a tribal ceremony, proudly faces the spectator. He expresses the pride of a tribal chieftain deeply conscious of his customs and heritage. The subject in the oil portrait of *Bungaree, a native of New South Wales. Fort, Sydney Harbour in the background* (no. 1) also stands in a noble attitude, facing the viewer. Earle has enhanced this impression of nobility by placing Bungaree close to the foreground and inserting a low-lying panorama (Sydney Harbour and Fort Macquarie) behind him, so that he dominates the painting. His arm is upraised and with a heroic, almost flamboyant, gesture he lifts his hat. While determined to exploit his position as a favourite of the Governor, Bungaree no doubt realised that many Europeans regarded him as a sort of licensed jester. There is an element of cynicism in his expression, and he seems aware of the fate of his race and the hopelessness and uncertainty of his position. In the lithographic version of this picture, no attempt has been made to elevate him. His face is thin and haggard and the cynical expression is more pronounced. His tattered trousers are a further reminder of his dependence upon the whites. Behind, one of his gins squats on the ground. On the right are grog bottles and rocks.

In these paintings, Earle conveys the slow degradation of the Aboriginal race proceeding during the period of his stay in Sydney. He demonstrates that it is the contact with European civilisation which is degrading these people. He not only realistically presents the Aborigines as they appeared at the time, but tries to understand their point of view.

A similar empiricism permeates Earle's descriptions of New Zealanders. He shows the Maoris in the midst of their daily chores, cleaning guns (*Two New Zealanders Squatting*, no. 136) or taking part in ceremonies and funerals (the studies of the dancers, nos 124 and 125; and *New Zealand Warriors and their Queen Trurero*, no. 121, and *Crying over the Bones of a Dead Chief. N. Zealand*, no. 140). Occasionally, as in the latter two pictures, nos 140 and 121, there is the same awkwardness in handling anatomical form which occurs in some of the Aboriginal studies, resulting in rather squat bodies and large heads. This is more than compensated for by the vigorous and lively use of expression and gesture. Earle's pen sketches of individual Maoris however exhibit the sharpness of observation evident in the Australian watercolours. In *New Zealanders, 3 figures* (no. 133), a few curving strokes gracefully outline a young girl, kneeling with her back to the viewer.

The refreshing spontaneity of these studies is achieved not only by sharp observation of their subjects' habits but by elimination of unnecessary detail. Earle has deftly interpreted the New Zealanders' weird postures;

they sit hunched into mounds, with their *kakahus* pulled around them in an effort to keep warm. He could not restrain himself from describing their occasionally comic appearance, blandly painting the rather absurd rear view of a *New Zealander in his common dress* (no. 132), who had quite unconsciously planted himself directly in front of the artist. The humorous incongruity presented by two Maoris earnestly muttering to one another in *Crying Party, New Zealand* (no. 131), while perfunctorily taking part in the wailing and slashing considered *de rigueur* at a funeral ceremony, no doubt delighted him. One view, showing two dark eyes peering furtively from the warmth of the *kakahu* (no. 133), the rest of the body indistinguishable beneath a cocoon of clothing, must also have appealed to Earle's sense of humour. These situations are so enthusiastically portrayed that they assume an anecdotal flavour; we can almost hear the conversation between the two warriors in no. 131.

These watercolours and drawings are essentially documentary in nature. They show Earle's curiosity about other customs and ways of life, a preoccupation evident in his journal. He respected the Maoris; they were hardworking and intelligent, and (unlike the Aborigines) had sought to profit from their contact with Europeans. 'I have often tried, in vain, to account for there being such a decided dissimilarity between the natives of New Holland and New Zealand . . . the natives of the latter island are "cast in beauty's perfect mould:" the children are so fine and powerfully made, that each might serve as a model for a statue of "the Infant Hercules:" nothing can exceed the graceful and athletic forms of the men, or the rounded limbs of their young women . . . while the intellects of both sexes seem of a superior order; all appear eager for improvement, full of energy, and indefatigably industrious. . . .'[67]

Four watercolour portraits (nos 126-9)[68] and several lithographs[69] indicate Earle's affection and respect for these people. In exquisitely subtle studies, generally enveloped in a soft atmospheric haze, he captures the particular mood and character of each individual. The Romantic overtones of the portraits link them to the nineteenth-century concept of the noble savage: 'As the noble savage had been an epitome of the virtues of the natural man of the Enlightenment[70] so the romantic savage became an epitome of the virtues treasured by the romantics.'[71] The characteristics of a Romantic savage were 'a great love of personal freedom, a devotion to race and "nation", a temperament which reacted violently and immediately to experience, courage, great emotional depth, and a childlike warmth and generosity of feeling . . . .'[72] These traits are mirrored in Earle's description of the Maoris: 'the New Zealander is quite a domestic, cheerful, harmless character: but once rouse his anger, or turn him into ridicule, and his

67 Earle, *Narrative* (1966), p.187.

68 That is, *A New Zealand Chief* (no. 126), *A New Zealand Chief from Terra Naky* (no. 127), *Amoko a New Zealand Girl* (no. 128), and *A New Zealander* (no. 129).

69 These include the two views of Heralds or Peacemakers, together with *Bay of Islands Chief, Herald or Peace-maker, Awow, Native Family* and the group portrait of *Amoko. Eana. Hepee.*, in *Sketches Illustrative of the Native Inhabitants and Islands of New Zealand, from Original Drawings* (London: R. Martin & Co., 1838).

70 For example, Hodges's classicised engravings of noble savages in New Zealand and Polynesia, c. 1777 (NLA).

71 Bernard Smith, *European Vision and the South Pacific, 1768-1850: A Study in the History of Art and Ideas* (Oxford: Clarendon Press, 1960), p.247.

72 Smith, *European Vision*, p.247.

Desmond, A New South Wales Chief
(No. 77 ; c.1825-7)

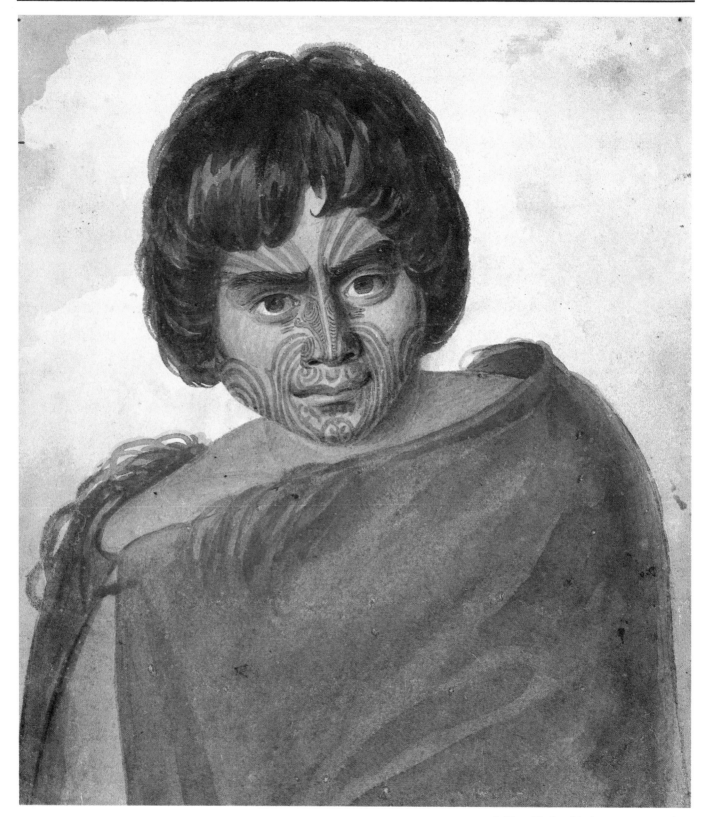

A New Zealander (no. 129; 1827-8)

disposition is instantly changed. A being, whose passions have never been curbed from infancy, . . . must naturally form a cruel and vindictive character.'[73]

The watercolours did arise of course out of Earle's desire to document the physical features and character of the New Zealanders, and it would be mistaken to suggest that he imposed upon them some preconceived notion of the Romantic savage. Rather, their childlike and passionate nature, coupled with their sensual beauty, have Romantic implications.

The watercolours nos 126-9 are basically accurate likenesses which attempt to suggest the character and mood of individuals. Careful draughtsmanship has been combined with subtle nuances of colour and tone in delineating the facial features. Earle pays particular attention to the eyes, especially the large, soulful eyes of the women Awow, Amoko, Eana and Hepee, to highlight their meditative, almost brooding, expressions. He also records the serious nature of many New Zealanders, as is evident in the intent expressions of the *Herald or Peace-maker* or *A New Zealander* (no. 129). At the same time, Earle conveys an impression of the innate dignity of these men. The natural warmth and affectionate nature of the Maoris is stressed in the lithograph of three young girls, *Amoko. Eana. Hepee,* and the rather more idealised view of a native family, which shows a child happily cuddling up to his parents. Mention should also be made of the evocative rendering of *A New Zealand Chief* (no. 126), in which careful brushstrokes describe the lovely skin, sensual mouth and large reflective eyes of the young man. The romantic atmosphere and lyrical quality of these watercolours is conveyed by the light, hazy backgrounds and soft shading around the outlined forms.

The pronounced narrative element in Earle's work is not surprising, given his intense curiosity and his interest in recording the occupations and customs of different peoples he encountered. The New Zealand paintings are often narratives of burial rites and ceremonies. In *Crying over the Bones of a Dead Chief. N. Zealand* (no. 140), the chief mourners sit in a circle chanting funeral dirges and moaning pitifully, while slashing their bodies with sharp instruments — the customary mark of respect for a dead chief. Another death scene, *New Zealand Warriors and their Queen Trurero* (no. 121), shows the grisly triumph with which victorious warriors present the impaled heads of conquered foes to Queen Turero. In the Australian watercolours, *Annual Meeting of Native Tribes at Paramatta* (no. 76) and the more exciting *Skirmish, Bush Rangers & Constables, Ilawarra* (no. 100) as well as the watercolours commemorating preliminary explorations of Mosman's Cave (nos 87-9) are of narrative interest.

Brazilian examples of this nature include *Don Pedro, as he appeared on his Coronation Day at Rio* (no. 30) and the savagely critical *Punishing Negroes at Cathabouco, Rio de Janeiro* (no. 22), which was no doubt painted with the anti-slavery movement in mind. It shows a Negro, his back branded with bloody weals, being whipped, watched with the utmost satisfaction by a white overseer, whose features are distorted into a caricature of cruelty. The impassive expressions of the prison attendants contrast with the agonised horror of the white spectator (the artist?), who covers his eyes in a gesture of revulsion. The stark stone walls and monotones of the painting heighten the intensity of the scene.

Tristan da Cunha also offered a wealth of narrative subject matter to the inquisitive artist. Earle records strenuous daily activities such as flinching

73 Earle, *Narrative* (1966), p.186.

yearling seals (no. 45), rafting blubber (no. 47), or hunting albatross along the mountain peaks above the 'village' (nos 49-50).

First sight of the Pacific Coast from America (no. 161) is more obviously drawn from eighteenth-century literary and historical sources. The rather restrained treatment of the foreground, and the use of expressive gestures, link the work generally with eighteenth-century engravings of a heroic nature depicting newly discovered lands. This drawing is further related to eighteenth-century anecdotal engravings, in that it is structured in such a way that one must 'read' the painting from left to right.

Within this large group comprising Earle's narrative paintings are works more closely linked with seventeenth-century Dutch and Flemish genre traditions; with eighteenth-century comic and anecdotal painting; and with the nineteenth-century rustic genre scenes like those by Sir David Wilkie and lesser-known provincial painters such as Joseph Parry and Edward Bird.[74] Three paintings in particular revive and amplify the low-life Dutch and Flemish genre paintings by Adriaen Van Ostade and Adriaen Brouwer. They are *Governor Glass & his Companions, Tristan D'Acunha* (no. 42), *Our Party while in the Island of Juan Fernandez* (no. 7), and *Extracting a Jiggar, Scene in the Brazils* (no. 26).

From about 1795, after the French Revolution, London became an important market for works of art. The stock of Dutch and Italian old masters was vastly increased. Dutch genre paintings also became much sought after by collectors and were in time shown in public exhibitions of old masters. Many of the great country houses, such as Houghton, Holsham and Wilton, held regular open days for the benefit of the general public. In 1815, the British Institution inaugurated its exhibitions of old masters and it is likely that Earle visited these showings. He would anyway have had ample opportunity to see the work of Dutch painters in some of the public and private collections. He would also have been familiar with the early work of Sir David Wilkie, the most popular painter of the day, whose early period was obviously influenced by seventeenth-century Dutch and Flemish genre painting. Earle must have seen Wilkie's Academy entries after *Village Politicians*, exhibited there in 1806, the same year as Earle's first showing. Wilkie later submitted *The Blind Fiddler*, *Village Festival* and *The Penny Wedding* and exhibited similar paintings at the British Institution in 1813-17.

Genre sources were widely available to English painters, and were greatly in demand from the turn of the century, leading to contemporary genre paintings by artists such as Wilkie. Earle's genre descriptions are however without the sentimental overtones of Wilkie's paintings. His ordinary, frequently grubby and unshaven characters are shown eating and drinking, with their shirt-sleeves rolled, buttons undone and legs outstretched, very much like their Dutch and Flemish antecedents. Often, in paintings such as *Negroes Fighting, Brazils* (no. 25), Earle deliberately includes a comic genre element, in this case the policeman awkwardly negotiating the fence. The livelier portrayals of Negroes dancing in *Negro Fandango Scene, Campo St. Anna nr. Rio* (no. 20) or the riotous antics of revellers in a brothel of *Games at Rio de Janeiro, during the Carnival* (no. 21) echo, too, the merrymaking and disorder described by the Dutch artists Jan Steen (in *The World Upside-Down*) and Breughel. Like those painters, Earle has the ability to grasp and

---

74 For illustrations of their work, *see* Trevor Fawcett, *The Rise of English Provincial Art: Artists, Patrons and Institutions outside London, 1800-1830* (Oxford: Clarendon Press, 1974).

Crying over the Bones of a Dead
Chief. N. Zealand (no. 140; 1828)

Governor Glass & his Companions,
Tristan D'Acunha (no. 42; 1824)

express the intrinsic quality — the folk or native element — of the scene to produce penetrating realistic descriptions of native life.

Two pen and wash drawings in Earle's collection illustrate scenes from novels by Tobias Smollett, *Scene from Peregrine Pickle* (no. 160) and *Scene from Roderick Random* (no. 159). Their relationship with engravings by Hogarth, Rowlandson and Cruikshank (still freely available at the beginning of the nineteenth century) is enhanced by the 'black and white' quality of the two monotone drawings. The mannerisms and movements of the characters, for example, the gentleman throwing up his hands in astonishment in no. 160, recall Hogarth's *Marriage a-la-Mode* or *The beggar's opera*.[75]

Earle employs a restrained, Hogarthian use of expression and gesture for comic effect, preferring it to the overt distortion of form employed by Gillray or Cruikshank. Such adroit handling of gesture and expression occurs throughout his *oeuvre*. Individual figures are frequently included for purely anecdotal or humorous detail, as in *From the Summit of the Cacavada Mountains, nr. Rio* (no. 15) or the unconventional positioning of the rather ridiculous-looking gentleman crouched on a rock in *View from the Summit of the South Head near Sidney* (no. 63). Such whims are endearing.

While the subject matter and approach in the maritime paintings (nos 12, 13, 14, 37 and 54)[76] are highly original, it is possible to see certain links with the two traditions described. The inclusion of humorous anecdotal elements and the lively delineation of facial expressions indicate a familiarity with eighteenth-century comic and anecdotal conventions, best shown in the humorous incongruity of the jack-in-the-box figure in the centre of *Midshipmens quarters on board a Ship of War* (no. 14), totally ignored by his fellow midshipmen. Earle also gives (in *Divine Service on Board a British Frigate*, no. 12) comic descriptions of the varying reactions, ranging from utter boredom to intense participation, aroused by the weekly sermon. The practical joking of midshipmen trying to pass the time in their cramped quarters is again typical of low-life genre scenes, and a strong documentary element is evident in the expressive and humorous attention to individual detail, as well as in the careful handling of the basic architectural framework.

Earle's choice of subject matter is however unusual. It seems that no other contemporary professional painter considered routine occurrences at sea as worthy of elaboration in finished paintings. Earle exhibited enlarged oil versions of *Midshipmens quarters on board a Ship of War* (no. 14) and *Divine Service on Board a British Frigate* (no. 12) at the Royal Academy in 1837. It is of course possible that other painters made quick sketches of these scenes to pass the time during voyages, but that these works have not come down to us. Apparently, most professional artists who travelled abroad were preoccupied with recording the abundant and more spectacular material available at the time in the scenery, flora and fauna of newly discovered lands. Later professional artists who travelled or emigrated were also more interested in recording strange and exotic phenomena. As well, the wars in Europe provided the artist with exciting material of greater interest to the people at home. Only after the middle of the century did genre-type scenes on board ship become popular, in lithographs or engravings published in contemporary journals and newspapers. The circulation of pictures of this nature increased

75 The jovial attitudes, coarse features and thickset bodies of the figures on the left in no. 159 also suggest parallels with Brouwer and Ostade.

76 That is, *On Board The Duke of Gloucester, South Atlantic* (no. 37), *Divine Service on Board a British Frigate* (no. 12), *Officers mess room on board a Ship of War* (no. 13) and *Midshipmens quarters on board a Ship of War* (no. 14).

with the growing number of emigrants to the colonies and the general interest in emigration. Settlers' letters and journals were being published, with accompanying illustrations. In exhibiting such early large-scale oil paintings of these scenes, Earle was highly innovatory, and extremely unusual.

Earle's originality

Earle's boundless curiosity and eager 'peregrinations and explorations' reflect the spirit of inquiry and expansion which characterised the nineteenth century. His ability to seek out and appreciate new and unusual material, and his unconventional situation as a roving freelance travel artist, were not wholly responsible however for the originality of his watercolours. His attitudes and general philosophy reflect the thought and ideals of the first half of the nineteenth century, relating both to contemporary advances in science and exploration and to current aesthetic ideas. Earle combines a Romantic response to nature with an acutely scientific interest in the accurate delineation of form. His empirical attitude led him to describe regional physiognomy as exactly as possible and, accordingly, to modify his technique to suit the particular demands of each place — the grim landforms of Tristan da Cunha, or the sleepy indolence of Guam.

In Australia at the time, this attitude of Earle's was both innovatory and unusual. As late as 1825, Barron Field[77] expressed in his *Geographical Memoirs on New South Wales* an eighteenth-century picturesque dissatisfaction with his surroundings. He complained that there was not a single scene in New South Wales 'of which a painter could make a landscape, without greatly disguising the true character of the trees'.[78] He laments the absence of 'lateral boughs' on trees which cast no shade, and has no words of admiration for the tropical vegetation of the Illawarra region. Artists in Australia tended to have the same view of nature as Field; the Australian landscape was to them hostile, monochrome and aesthetically unpleasing. Yearning for England, they painted Australia as if it were England. They were unwilling, rather than unable, to grasp the regional and material peculiarities of the bush or to appreciate the peculiar colour, texture and sparseness of the trees.

This attitude marks the work of Joseph Lycett, a convict who arrived in Australia in 1814. In his painting, he modified the scenery according to picturesque conventions, so that his views of the country would appeal to the taste of his public at home in England. He was either reluctant or unable to grasp such peculiarities of the Australian bush as the open foliage of eucalyptus trees, which permits glimpses of the scenery behind. Instead, Lycett's generalised definitions of trees were densely clumped together and were painted in uncharacteristically bright yellows and greens, with a rather naive approach to form and detail. One artist who did share Earle's naturalistic attitude to landscape was John Lewin (c. 1769-1819), who landed at Sydney in 1800. His watercolours of the Blue Mountains attempt to capture the open nature of the Australian trees and their indigenous olive-blue colour, and to suggest also the sparseness of the Australian landscape. Yet, despite his more naturalistic interpretation, Lewin was not as accomplished an artist as Earle. There is a slightly amateurish quality in his work, possibly because he was never trained, which is evident in his occasionally awkward attempts to render

77 Field was appointed a Supreme Court Judge of New South Wales in 1816. He published *First Fruits of Australian Poetry* (Sydney: 1819) in 1819 and *Geographical Memoirs on New South Wales, by various hands . . .* (London: John Murray, 1825) in 1825.
78 Field, *Geographical Memoirs*, p.422.

Negro Fandango Scene, Campo St.
Anna nr. Rio (no. 20; 1821-4)

depth. Nor was he as adept as Earle at conveying the atmosphere and character of particular regions.

Earle's paintings are valuable, then, both as works of art and as documentary records of historic and ethnographic significance. He effectively describes not only the external features of places he visited, but also conveys something of their character and atmosphere; there is always an underlying human element in his paintings. This has meant that scholars, students and admirers in Brazil, Australia and New Zealand all claim him as *their* country's artist — an enduring tribute.

Officers Mess Room on board a Ship
of War (no. 13; 1820-1)

The plates

It is likely that Earle painted the watercolours in the Rex Nan Kivell Collection with the intention of publishing them either as a volume of aquatints, as several volumes illustrating his travels, or possibly as companion illustrations for his unpublished *Voyage Round the World*, mentioned in the original manuscript list of numbers and titles which accompanied the paintings.

Most of the works are numbered and titled on the mount from 1 to 165, and are prefaced by the Nan Kivell location symbol 'NK 12/'. The numbering of the paintings is quite arbitrary and relates to the accompanying manuscript list. There are no items for numbers NK 12/12, NK 12/18, NK 12/111 and NK 12/161, although the last is described on the manuscript list as *Portrait of Lord Cochrane drawn at Rio in 1824*. This work was not included in the collection when it was acquired by Rex Nan Kivell. There is no manuscript entry for the titles of nos NK 12/135 and NK 12/157, and NK 12/165 is unrecorded in the manuscript list. Titles are taken from the manuscript list, but there are minor differences between the titles as recorded on the list and as written on the mounts. It seems likely that the titles on the mounting sheets and the manuscript list, both written in a hand other than Earle's,[1] were completed before Earle's death, perhaps under his supervision.

The plates have been arranged in chronological order, as far as this was possible to establish, and the Nan Kivell sequence has been adhered to within the chronological order where possible. For ease of reference to the plates running numbers have been added and all references in the text are to these. As all the paintings in the collection are reproduced here, the notes accompanying the plates are intended to be explanatory rather than descriptive in nature. The inscription records the title of the painting as written on the mounting sheets, and where Earle wrote on the reverse of the painting, this has been noted. Notes of any kind which appear on the surface of the painting have been recorded from left to right. For reference purposes the correct spelling of place names has been included in square brackets.

Because of the arbitrary nature of the Nan Kivell numbers, many scholars have assumed that Earle not only mounted, numbered and added titles to these paintings, but that he also painted all the watercolours when he returned to England. However, there is evidence to suggest that many of the watercolours were painted during Earle's travels. Their freshness and immediacy indicates an immediate setting down. Only recently has new information come to light to support this judgment. A thorough examination of the surface of each watercolour provided informative data such as previously indistinguishable colour notes and annotations, which prompted a further, more comprehensive, examination. The mount sheets were removed and the back of each painting was checked for further information. On the reverse of some of the watercolours, Earle had added further explanatory details such as that on the

---

1 In June 1975, a handwriting expert from the Commonwealth Police Force concluded that the inscriptions on the mounts were not written by Earle.

reverse of no. 42 (*Governor Glass & his Companions, Tristan D'Acunha*), where he wrote, 'The Gov.r is lighting his pipe.' This note helped to isolate and identify some of the people in the painting. Pencil drawings were also found on the back of some of the watercolours (nos 17, 18, 39 and 155). These discoveries add a further dimension to analysis of Earle's style, and contribute to the interest and value of the paintings.

The poor quality of the paper available to Earle necessitated reinforcement. Earle seems to have used any material he found for this purpose, backing the paintings with pages torn from log-books and naval reference books. When the National Library's conservator removed successive backing sheets (some of the paintings having been reinforced with two or three sheets of paper), further related material was discovered.

It is worthwhile to assess these findings more specifically, to establish whether the watercolours were painted during the artist's travels. If Earle had repainted all the watercolours when he returned to London, he would not have found it necessary to repeat the colour notes and annotations which occur on many of the paintings.[2] Rather, he would have worked from the original sketches, taking note of the colours already on the paintings. In some cases, however, he made careful note of the title, location or compass bearing (as in no. 8) and time of depiction (as in nos 31, 34, 35, 139 and 152). Such works can only have been painted on the spot or, where there are colour notes alone, may have been completed shortly afterwards. Conclusive evidence is provided in paintings such as no. 139, where Earle provides contemporary data together with his signature: 'The E.O. Racky, or Deptford Dockyard, on the E.O. Keangha River. N. Zealand, sketched in 1828/A. Earle.' If Earle had painted the watercolours on his return home, he would doubtless have used fresh, good-quality paper. Reinforcement would not have been necessary; and, given the wide variety of different papers available in London for reinforcement purposes, it is doubtful if he would have chosen material such as the sheets taken from log-books which remained the property of His Majesty's Navy, particularly as the watercolours were intended for reproduction. Nor is it likely that Earle would have used paper with pencil sketches on the reverse; or (as in no. 28, *A Sleeping Negro, Brazils — No. 2*) that he would have included a work with the obliterated sketch of a column base still visible on the right of the painting. The unfinished nature of some of the watercolours, mostly portraits, also suggests on-the-spot execution (*see* nos 65, 164 and 166). *Portrait of a Lady* (no. 164) is particularly interesting; a considerable area of the picture has been left blank.

Earle probably painted some of the Tristan da Cunha watercolours during his sojourn on the island. A shortage of paper, however, compelled him to repaint some of the sketches on the *Admiral Cockburn* en route to Australia. Occasional reminders of colour (nos 47 and 51), together with certain improvisations carried out to enlarge the size of the paper, by attaching a narrow strip around the borders (as in no. 48), suggest that these paintings at least were painted on the island. In his journal, the artist unhappily records his diminishing stock of paper and laments that no other material on the island is suitable for drawing purposes. He was obliged, therefore, to cover both sides. 'As long as my paper and pencils lasted, they were a source of infinite amusement; but now, alas! all are entirely used, and sketches made on both sides of my paper . . . I must economise, and am thus cut off from one of my chief sources of occupation.'[3]

2 That is, nos 18, 32, 47, 51, 67, 76, 78, 83, 90, 105, 107, 112, 139, 149, 150 and 152.
3 Earle, *Journal* (1966), p.234.

Since none of the extant watercolours was painted on both sides, it must be assumed that Earle repainted them shortly afterwards. He undoubtedly reinforced the paintings with paper found on board, such as the log-books, naval reference books and navigational exercises described earlier, which could only have been found on a ship. Nos 46 and 48 are attached to sheets of paper taken from a log-book. The former is unusually intriguing; letters of the alphabet have been transcribed in a childish hand over the ship's entries. We know that Earle gave lessons to the Glass children on the island.[4] However, in this case, he probably used old pieces of paper found on the *Admiral Cockburn* and used by the Walker children, who were passengers during this voyage, to practise upon.[5]

One can imagine Earle filling in the long hours at sea painting, then laboriously attaching extra material to his watercolours. He may even have attempted to tutor the unruly Walker children; a wearying task if indeed the boy tickling the artist in no. 54 was a member of the family. No. 40 is glued to three sheets of paper, two of which describe different standards of weights and measures used in foreign countries. The third page comprises a log-book entry. No. 37 is attached to more technically navigational material: a sheet taken from an officer's exercise book, containing a written explanation and an equation determining the ship's position using the moon's aspect. No doubt there was a plentiful supply of such material on board ship, and a store of artist's materials for the officers.

Abbreviations

NLA	National Library of Australia
ML	Mitchell Library
NK	Nan Kivell
Inscr.	Inscribed
l.l.	Occurring on the lower left surface of painting
l.c.	Lower centre
l.r.	Lower right
u.l.	Upper left
u.c.	Upper centre
u.r.	Upper right
t.l.	Top left
t.c.	Top centre
t.r.	Top right

4 Earle, *Journal* (1966), p.211.
5 *Sydney Gazette*, 3 March 1825.

Oil paintings

1 Bungaree, a native of New South Wales. Fort, Sydney Harbour in the background (c. 1826) (NK 118)

Unsigned and undated
Oil on canvas 68.5 x 51 cm
Exhibited Rex Nan Kivell Collection Exhibition. NLA, 1974

Notes

Earle also executed a lithograph of Bungaree in his *Views in New South Wales and Van Diemen's Land* (Part II, Plate I). The lithograph was possibly based on this work and accompanying watercolour sketches (now lost). Part of the text to this plate reads 'One of the first people generally seen after landing, is BUNGAREE, a Native Chief. He is generally aware of the arrival of strangers, and stations himself in as conspicuous a situation as possible, and welcomes them into his Country.

'This harmless savage, is Chief of a tribe which occupied the country round Sydney, previous to its being settled by us . . . . Governor Macquarrie took great pains with this man and his tribe . . . . but all was of no avail . . . . The only presents Bungaree retained, and which he sets great store by, are an old cocked hat, and a general's uniform. These people (and particularly this man) are great mimics, and the graceful bow he makes to strangers he copied from one of the Governors, and those who recollect the original, say it is exact.

'The accompanying likeness represents him in the act taking off his hat and bowing to the strangers landing.'

McGarvie saw the portrait in Earle's gallery in October 1826 and wrote in the *Sydney Gazette* of 30 July 1829 'Bungarie, chief of the Broken Bay tribe of blacks, in his usual dress, a blue surcoat, cocked hat, and brass plate on his breast.' In the background is a view of Sydney Harbour, including Fort Macquarie.

2 Bougainville Falls, Prince Regents Glen, Blue Mountains N.S.W. (c. 1826-7) (NK 9)

Oil on canvas	Unsigned and undated 71.1 x 83.2 cm
Exhibited	Australian Painting, XIX and XX Century. Auckland, 1964. Exhibition assembled by the Commonwealth Arts Advisory Board

Notes
The artist is shown seated in the foreground, drawing one of his Aboriginal guides.

3 A Bivouac of Travellers in Australia, in a Cabbage-tree Forest, day break
(c. 1838) (NK 14)

	Unsigned and undated
Oil on canvas	118.1 x 81.9 cm
Exhibited	Rex Nan Kivell Collection Exhibition. NLA, 1974

Notes

Earle exhibited a painting of the same title at the Royal Academy in 1838 (*see* Algernon Graves, *The Royal Academy of Arts. A Complete Dictionary of Contributors and their work from its foundation in 1769 to 1904* (Bath: Kingsmead Reprints, 1969), v.3, p.4. However, as that painting was hung in the miniatures and small paintings room at the Academy, it is possible that Earle painted a smaller version (now lost) and exhibited it in 1838.

Four watercolours in the Rex Nan Kivell Collection (nos 93-6) also depict scenes in the Illawarra district, which Earle visited in April-May 1827. The oil would appear to be based directly on no. 95, *A Bivouack, day break, on the Ilawarra Mountains.*

4 Maori being Tattooed by a Maori in front of a Whare (Date unknown)
(NK 1106)

Unsigned and undated
Oil on canvas 50.8 x 61 cm
Exhibited Early Watercolours of New Zealand. Auckland City Art Gallery, 1963

Notes

Reproduced in Earle's *A Narrative of a Nine Months' Residence in New Zealand in 1827 . . .* (1832), facing p.136 as *New Zealand method of Tattooing.*

This is one of the few paintings in which a Maori is depicted inside a hut or 'whare' (*see also* the watercolour no. 120). These buildings were small, about one metre in height and three metres across, necessitating the reclining attitude of the native in the painting. To the right of the hut a bag of food hangs from a wooden pole (*see* Notes, no. 110).

The identity of the tattooer in the foreground is not known. He bears little resemblance to the famous Aranghie depicted in the watercolour (no. 129).

'The art of tattooing has been brought to such perfection here, that whenever we have seen a New Zealander whose skin is thus ornamented, we have admired him. It is looked upon as answering the same purposes as clothes. When a chief throws off his mats, he seems as proud of displaying the beautiful ornaments figured on his skin, as a first rate exquisite is in exhibiting himself in his last fashionable attire. It is an essential part of warlike preparations.' (Earle, *Narrative* (1966), p.124).

5 Attributed to Augustus Earle
Maori with Pipe (Date unknown)
(NK 1320)
                    Unsigned and undated
Oil on canvas 35.6 x 25.4 cm
Notes
    Portrait extensively retouched around
back of head. The manner in which the
subject has been portrayed suggests a
mid-nineteenth century (that is, after
Earle's death) date and thus it is
doubtful if the portrait was painted by
him.

Watercolours

6 General View of the Island of Juan Fernandez (1820) (NK 12/91)

Inscription   '91. A general view of the Island of Juan Fernandes' on mount

Watercolour   13 x 77.8 cm
In five sections, backed with cloth and folded. The three centre sections mounted on cardboard

Notes

Juan Fernández is the name given to a group of three islands, Más a Tierra, Más Afuera and Santa Clara, in the South Pacific Ocean approximately 650 km west of Chile. They were discovered in 1563 by Juan Fernández, a Spanish navigator. Sovereignty passed to Chile when it won independence in 1818. Alexander Selkirk, who remained on Más a Tierra from 1704 to 1709, was the original model for Daniel Defoe's *The Life and Strange Surprising Adventures of Robinson Crusoe* (London: Elliot Stock, 1883). *See also* no. 162.

7 Our Party while in the Island of Juan Fernandez (1820) (NK 12/92)

Inscription	'92. View of our Party during our residence on the Island of Juan Fernandez' on mount
Reverse	'View of our party — During our residence at the Island of Juan Fernandes'
Watercolour	26.1 x 38.1 cm Dark mould spots on surface indicate that these areas have been retouched
Exhibited	Rex Nan Kivell Collection Exhibition. NLA, 1974

Notes

Unfortunately there is no evidence to suggest the identity of 'our party'.

8 Isle Evouts, near Cape Horne, bearing N.W. by W. (1820) (NK 12/109)

Inscription	'109. Isle Evouts; near Cape Horn, bearing N.W. by W. by Compass' (u.l.) in ink
Reverse	'N'
Black and white tonal watercolour	11.1 x 16.2 cm

Notes

The Isle of Evouts is a small island about 30 km southeast of Cape Horn. The unembellished nature of the drawing and the inclusion of the compass bearing suggests that this is a topographical coastal view, similar to those made by navigators during surveying expeditions.

9 Cape St. John, Staten Land, breakers appearing (1820) (NK 12/110)

Inscription — '110. Cape St. John, Staten land, with the appearance of breakers, as seen from Deck, May 15th 1820' (u.c.) in ink

Black and white tonal watercolour — 12.7 x 50.8 cm

Notes

Staten Island is 25 km northeast of Cape Horn. Earle would have passed the island in May 1820 on his way to Chile and Peru.

10 Lima (Late 1820) (NK 12/113)

Inscription   '1 Lima' (l.c.), '2 Callao'
                (l.c.), '3 Island of St.
                Lorenzo' (l.r.), '1' (u.c.),
                '2' (u.c.), '3' (u.r.)
Watercolour   14.6 x 218.4 cm
                In five sections. Mounted
                on cloth. Numerous folds
                and creases

Notes

The length of the work, together with the system of numbering and annotation, indicates that it was intended as a study for a panorama.

Earle was in Lima from July–December 1820. This painting is historically significant, as it commemorates Lord Cochrane's blockade of the harbour of Callao (5 November 1820). In the painting the ships pictured near San Lorenzo (25 km west of Lima) fly the Chilean flag, while those in the harbour at Callao, like the fort on shore, fly the Spanish ensign.

Earle left Lima just after the blockade. He sailed from Callao on 10 December on board the *Hyperion*. The *Hyperion* sheltered many Englishmen during the blockade, and it is probable that Earle witnessed the event.

11 View of the City of Lima, the Plains of Remac [Rimac] & the Andes (1820) (NK 12/114)

Inscription   '114. View of the city of Lima, the plains of Remac, & a distant view of the Andes' on mount

Watercolour   15.2 x 53 cm
Exhibited   Rex Nan Kivell Collection Exhibition. NLA, 1974
Notes
  The Rimac River flows from the Andes west to the city of Lima and thence to the Pacific Ocean.

12 Divine Service on Board a British Frigate (1820) (NK 12/130)

Inscription   '130. Divine Service on board a British Frigate, H.M.S. *Hyperion* 1820' on mount

Watercolour   17.1 x 30.5 cm
Exhibited   Rex Nan Kivell Collection Exhibition. NLA, 1974
Notes
  This watercolour was no doubt the basis for the oil painting (now in the National Maritime Museum, Greenwich) exhibited at the Royal Academy in 1837, entitled *Divine Service, as it is usually performed on board a British frigate at sea.*

  H.M.S. *Hyperion* was in Callao during Lord Cochrane's blockade of the harbour in 1820 (*see* no. 10). Earle left Callao on board the *Hyperion* on 10 December 1820.

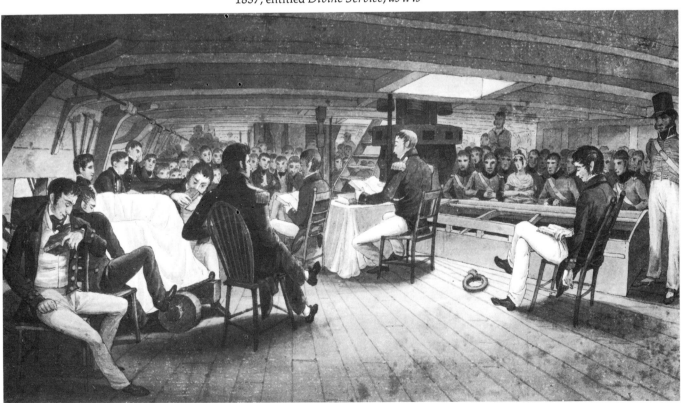

13 Officers Mess Room on board a Ship of War (1820-1) (NK 12/131)

Inscription	'131. Officers Mess Room on board a Ship of War' on mount
Reverse	'Officers Mess room on board an . . .' [ship of war? remaining title cut off]
Watercolour	20 x 30.2 cm Scratches on surface for highlights
Exhibited	Rex Nan Kivell Collection Exhibition. NLA, 1974

Notes

This work is similar in character to no. 12 and may (with no. 14) have been intended to form part of a series depicting life on board H.M.S. *Hyperion*.

14 Midshipmens quarters on board a Ship of War (1820-1) (NK 12/132)

Inscription	'132. View of the Mid-shipmens Quarters on board a Ship of War' on mount
Reverse	'View of the Midshipmens quarters on board a ship of War No. 17' in ink
Watercolour	17.5 x 33.3 cm
Exhibited	Rex Nan Kivell Collection Exhibition. NLA, 1974

Notes

Possibly another of a series illustrating life on board H.M.S. *Hyperion*. The watercolour is related to the oil painting *The gun room in a man-of-war* (in the National Maritime Museum, Greenwich), attributed to Earle by H.E. Spencer in September 1964. In 1837 Earle exhibited a painting at the Royal Academy entitled *Life on the ocean, representing the usual occupation of the young officers in the steerage of a British frigate at sea* (see Graves, *The Royal Academy of Arts*, v.3, p.3).

15 From the Summit of the Cacavada [Corcovado] Mountains, nr. Rio (1821-4) (NK 12/93)

Inscription	'93. View from the Summit of the Cacavada Mountains Near Rio de Janeiro'
Reverse	'View from the summit of the Cocovada Mountain near Rio de Janeiro'
Watercolour	20.3 x 33.7 cm
Exhibited	Rex Nan Kivell Collection Exhibition. NLA, 1974

Notes

The famous Sugar Loaf rock is situated on the right (middle-ground). In the distance (t.l.) is the Corcovado, the highest point in the surrounding mountain chain of the same name, which today is surmounted by a monumental statue of Christ.

16 Rio de Janeiro Bay, Lord Cochranes Boat and Crew (1824) (NK 12/94)

Inscription	'94. View of the Bay of Rio de Janeiro, Lord Cochrane's Boat & Crew' on mount
Reverse	'View in the Bay of Rio de Janeiro Lord Cochrane's boat & Boatcrew'
Watercolour	17.5 x 26 cm Scratches on surface to indicate highlights
Exhibited	Rex Nan Kivell Collection Exhibition. NLA, 1974

Notes

Lord Cochrane was one of the most brilliant naval commanders of the period. In 1817 he was invited by the Chilean Government to command the navy in its war of independence against Spain. On 21 March 1823, Don Pedro engaged him to command the Brazilian fleets, drive out the Portuguese garrisons from Brazil and subdue the rebellious provinces of the north, Bahia, Pará and Maranhao. Cochrane effectively carried out his commission by September of the same year.

The Dois Irmaos, or Two Brothers, Mountain is visible in the right background.

17 View near Rio de Janeiro (1821-4)
(NK 12/95)

Inscription	'95. Near Rio de Janeiro' on mount
Reverse	'Near Rio de Janeiro'. Small pencil sketch of Rio de Janeiro bay with mountains in the background. In the foreground (l.r.) is a boat with four men
Watercolour	17.1 x 25.6 cm Scratches on surface of water to indicate ripples
Exhibited	Rex Nan Kivell Collection Exhibition. NLA, 1974

Notes

The view is of one of the many inlets in the Bay at Rio de Janeiro. Earle originally intended the fisherman's arm (l.c.) to be outstretched in the direction of the bay — the previous outline is faintly discernible — but later altered it.

18 View near Rio de Janeiro (1821-4)
(NK 12/96)

Inscription	'96. View near Rio de Janeiro' on mount. L. to r. 'light' (u.r.), 'Dark' (u.r.)
Reverse	Pencil sketch of a large boat moored in the foreground (u.c.) with a smaller vessel (l.c.) also moored in the harbour. Mountains in the distance
Watercolour	17.8 x 26 cm Scratches in creek to indicate current
Exhibited	Rex Nan Kivell Collection Exhibition. NLA, 1974

Notes

The view is of the Laranjeiras Valley, situated on the outskirts of Rio. 'Just at the entrance to that valley, a little green plain stretches itself on either hand, through which the rivulet runs over its stony bed, and affords a tempting spot to groups of washerwomen . . . they generally wear a red or white handkerchief round the head; and a full plaited mantle tied over one shoulder, and passed under the opposite arm . . . some wrap a long cloth round them, like the Hindoos' (Graham, *Journal of a Voyage to Brazil* [New York: Frederick A. Praeger, 1969], p. 161).

19 The Banana, Brazils (1821-4)
(NK 12/97)

Inscription	'97. The Banana, Brazils' on mount
Reverse	'The Banana. Brazils'
Watercolour	18.4 x 12.7 cm Scratches in paint to highlight natives' clothing.

20 Negro Fandango Scene, Campo St. Anna nr. Rio (1821-4) (NK 12/98)

Inscription	'98. Negro Fandango Scene, Campo St. Anna Rio de Janeiro' on mount
Reverse	'Negroe. F'andango, Scene, Campo St. Anna, Rio de Janeiro'
Watercolour	21 x 34 cm
Exhibited	Rex Nan Kivell Collection Exhibition. NLA, 1974

Notes

The scene shows a primitive dance (probably the Batuque or Batuca) taking place in front of vendors' stalls.

21 Games at Rio de Janeiro, during the Carnival (1821-4) (NK 12/99)

Inscription	'99. Games during the Carnival at Rio de Janeiro' on mount
Watercolour	21.6 x 34 cm
Exhibited	Rex Nan Kivell Collection Exhibition. NLA, 1974

Notes

Carnival celebrants are making merry in an elegant Rio brothel. An intrudo ball battle is being waged with the neighbours across the street. These intrudo balls consist of shells of wax filled with water, which explode as soon as they hit their target. The balls are shaped and coloured to resemble fruit.

22 Punishing Negroes at Cathabouco [Calobouco], Rio de Janeiro (1821-4)
(NK 12/100)

Inscription   '100. Punishing Negroes
              at Cathabouco Rio de
              Janeiro' on mount
Reverse   'Punishing Negroes at the
              Cathabouco, Rio de
              Janeiro'
Watercolour   23.5 x 26 cm

Notes

For a minor offence, Negro slaves could be dragged off to Calobouco, the prison for blacks. 'Their owners procure an order from the intendant-general of the police, for one, two, or three hundred lashes, according to the dictates of their caprice or passion, which punishment is administered to those poor wretches by one of their own countrymen, a stout,

savage-looking, degraded Negro' (James Henderson, *A history of the Brazil comprising its Geography, Commerce, Colonization, Aboriginal Inhabitants &c.* [London: Longman, 1821], p. 72) quoted in H. E. Spencer, *Augustus Earle: a Study of Early Nineteenth Century Travel Art and its Place in English Landscape and Genre Traditions* [Harvard, 1967], p. 142-3.

23 Rita a Celebrated Black Beauty at Rio de Janeiro (1821-4) (NK 12/101)

Inscription   '101. Rita, a celebrated
                  Black Beauty at Rio de
                  Janeiro' on mount
Reverse   'Rita, a celebrated Black
                  beauty at Rio de Janeiro'
Watercolour   28.9 x 20 cm
Exhibited   Rex Nan Kivell Collection
                  Exhibition. NLA, 1974

Notes

Rita's pose is similar to that used earlier by the neoclassic artist Girodet in his portrait of the Negro deputy J. J. Belley in 1793-4 (*see* Jack Lindsay, *Death of the Hero: French Painting from David to Delacroix* [London: Studio, 1961], plate 118).

24 An Eccliastic [sic] of Rio de Janeiro
(1821-4) (NK 12/102)
Inscription   '102. An Ecclesiastic of
                 Rio de Janeiro' on mount
Watercolour   31.1 x 17.8 cm
Exhibited   Rex Nan Kivell Collection
                 Exhibition. NLA, 1974
Notes
  The high conical hat with a wide brim
was typical of those worn by the clergy
in Rio.

25 Negroes Fighting, Brazils (1821-4)
(NK 12/103)

Inscription	'103. Negroes Fighting, Brazils' on mount
Reverse	'Negroes fighting, Brazils'
Watercolour	16.5 x 25.1 cm
Exhibited	Rex Nan Kivell Collection Exhibition. NLA, 1974

Notes

A colonial policeman is climbing over the fence to stop the two Negroes engaged in the Capoeira, or 'headbumping', game. The object of the game is to knock one's opponent down by bumping him in the chest with the head. According to contemporary sources, the participants sometimes collided head on, causing the game to degenerate into a brawl.

26 Extracting a Jiggar, Scene in the Brazils (1821-4) (NK 12/104)

Inscription	'104. Extracting a Jigger, Scene in the Brazils' on mount
Reverse	'Extracting a Gigger, Scene in Brazils'
Watercolour	20.3 x 21 cm
Exhibited	Rex Nan Kivell Collection Exhibition. NLA, 1974

Notes

'Jigger' is the common name of a small flea that burrows beneath the skin of man in tropical America and Africa, southern United States and India. It most frequently penetrates the tender skin between the toes. Treatment consists of removing the flea and cleansing the wound. The man seated has evidently been attacked, as the coloured maid is extracting the jigger flea from his foot.

27 A Sleeping Negro Brazils — No. 1
(1821-4) (NK 12/105)
Inscription   '105. A Sleeping Negro,
                  Brazils' on mount
Watercolour   19.4 x 17.8 cm
Exhibited   Rex Nan Kivell Collection
                  Exhibition. NLA, 1974.

28 A Sleeping Negro, Brazils – No. 2
(1821-4) (NK 12/106)
Inscription   '106. A Sleeping Negro,
                 Brazils' on mount
                 'A Sleeping Negroe.
                 Brazils' in ink (l.c.)
                 Faint pencil outline of a
                 column base (u.r.)

Watercolour 18.1 x 21.3 cm
Exhibited   Rex Nan Kivell Collection
             Exhibition. NLA, 1974.

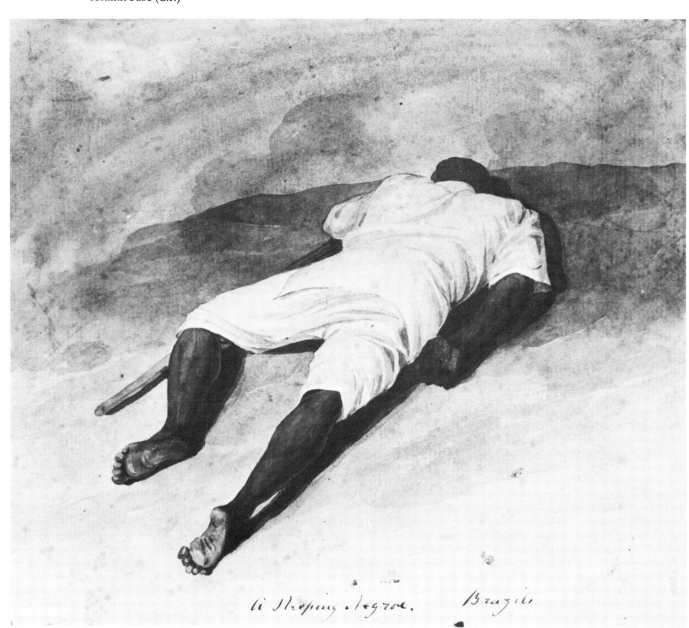

29 Portrait of the Riding Master to the Empress, Brazils (c. 1822) (NK 12/107)

Inscription	'107. Riding Master to the Empress of the Brazils' on mount 'Riding Master to the Empress of Bra . . . ' (l.r.) in pencil, [. . . ?] (t.r.), [. . . ?] (l.r.)
Reverse	Pencil sketch of a horse and rider
Watercolour	21.6 x 14.9 cm
Exhibited	Rex Nan Kivell Collection Exhibition. NLA, 1974.

30 Don Pedro, as he appeared on his Coronation Day at Rio (1822)
(NK 12/108)

Inscription	'108. Don Pedro as he appeared on the day of his Coronation at Rio de Janeiro' on mount
Watercolour	15.6 x 11.1 cm
Exhibited	Rex Nan Kivell Collection Exhibition. NLA, 1974

Notes

The royal family of Portugal fled to Brazil in 1808, and for 13 years Brazil was the headquarters of the Portuguese Empire. In 1821 John VI returned to Lisbon, leaving his son Pedro to act as regent. Supported by the majority of Brazilians, Pedro I (pictured) defied the orders of the Cortes Government in Portugal. In January 1822, he formed a ministry and on 3 June convoked a legislative and constituent assembly. He proclaimed the independence of Brazil on 7 September and was crowned emperor on 1 December 1822.

31 The Bat of Brazils, 26 Inches Long (1822) (NK 12/112)

Inscription	'112. The Bat of Brazils, 26 Inches long. Campos March 17th 1822' (l.r.) in ink
Watercolour	21.6 x 50.8 cm
Exhibited	Rex Nan Kivell Collection Exhibition. NLA, 1974

Notes

The precision displayed in this natural history drawing, together with the specific accompanying note, suggests that Earle may have received odd commissions from scientists or scholars while in Brazil. Campos is a town 250 km northeast of Rio.

32 The River and Town of St. Juan
(1821-4) (NK 12/115)
Inscription   '115. The River and Town
               of St. Juan' (l.c.), 'Cape
               Frio' (l.r.) in ink on mount
               l. to r. 'Desert' [?] (t.c.),
               'light' [?] (t.r.), [. . . ?]
               (t.r.)

Watercolour   10.2 x 59.5 cm
               In four sections. Narrow
               horizontal strip along top
               of painting. Extensive
               mould. Fading along right
               and left edges

Notes
    Cape Frio is 100 km northeast of Rio.

33 Cocoa Tree Brazils (1821-4)
(NK 12/123)

Inscription	'123. Cocoa Tree Brazils' on mount
Reverse	'Cocoa Nut Tree Brazils'
Watercolour	18.4 x 11.1 cm in ink

Notes

Caption beneath painting should read 'Cocoanut', not 'cocoa', since this is a coconut tree. Behind the tree is a typical Brazilian bungalow. In the background is the Dois Irmaos (Two Brothers) Mountain, together with the Gávea rock.

34 Costume of the Brazils, man on horseback & 4 figures (1824)
(NK 12/154)

Inscription	'154' in ink. 'Costume of Brazils' (u.c.) in pencil '1824 Slave Selling sweetmeats' (l.l.) 'Padre' (l.l.) 'Mineroes [Miners]' (l.r.) in pencil
Pencil	14.9 x 29.2 cm

35 Costume of Brazils, 4 figures (1824)
(NK 12/155)

Inscription	'155' (in ink), 'Costume of Brazils' (u.c.), '1824' (l.l.), 'Brazilian Ladies' (l.l.), 'Sweetmeats' (l.r.), 'Vegetables' (l.r.) in pencil
Pencil	15.2 x 27.9 cm

**36 Female Soldier of South America, a
Portrait** (1824) (NK 12/162)

Inscription   '162. A Female Soldier of
                   South America'
Reverse   'A Woman Soldier'
Watercolour   17.1 x 14.3 cm
Notes

The young woman is Dona Maria de
Jesus. She served with distinction in the
Brazilian infantry during Brazil's struggle
for independence from Portugal in
March-September 1822. Earle also drew
a full-length portrait of Dona Maria
which was engraved by Edward Finden,
as an illustration for Maria Graham's
Journal of a Voyage to Brazil (1969),
plate 10. In it she is wearing the Order
of the Cross conferred upon her by the
Emperor Pedro I.

37 On Board The Duke of Gloucester, South Atlantic (1824) (NK 12/1)

Inscription	'1. On Board The Duke of Gloucester, Margate Hoy, between Rio de Janeiro and Tristan De Acunha in the South Atlantic' on mount
Reverse	'On board the Duke of Gloster Margate Hoy/ between Rio de Janeiro and Tristan de Acunha' Backed with two pages torn from an officer's exercise book, filled with equations which attempt to define the exact position of the vessel using the aspect of the moon
Watercolour	17.5 x 25.7 cm
Exhibited	Rex Nan Kivell Collection Exhibition. NLA, 1974

Notes

The presence of the log-book on the table suggests that one of the men may be Captain Ham — possibly the figure on the left, since the right-hand figure resembles the self-portrait of Earle in no. 39.

Earle boarded the *Duke of Gloucester*, bound for the Cape of Good Hope, on 17 February 1824 at Rio de Janeiro. After some weeks of extremely treacherous weather culminating in prolonged storms and squalls, the overladen vessel was forced to anchor on 26 March off Tristan da Cunha.

Tristan da Cunha is the largest, and only populated, island in a group of three in the south Atlantic ocean, the other two islands being Nightingale and Inaccessible, which are respectively 27 km south and 32 km south-west of Tristan da Cunha. It is farther from populated land than any other island in the world, being 2900 km west of the Cape of Good Hope and 2880 km from the coast of Uruguay.

Earle's journal reads:
'We hove to about a mile from the shore, . . . and these settlers seemed most happy at our arrival, as ships so very seldom can touch here. . . . I determined to return in the boat with the men when they left our vessel: I did so, and took with me my dog, gun, boat cloak, and sketch book, hoping to be able to add a few interesting drawings to my portfolio. . . .' (Earle, *Journal* [1966], p.205). Earle was left stranded on the island on 29 March, with a sailor from the *Duke of Gloucester*, Thomas Gooch, when the vessel suddenly tacked and made for the open sea.

38 Government House, Tristan D'Acunha (1824) (NK 12/2)

Inscription	'2. Government House. Tristan De Acunha' on mount
Reverse	'Government House Tristan de Acunha'
Watercolour	17.5 x 26 cm
Exhibited	Rex Nan Kivell Collection Exhibition. NLA, 1974 Reproduced with minor omissions in Earle's journal, published in 1832 and engraved by J. Stewart. The wooden tub

(u.r.) and the dog (l.c.) were not included in the engraving

Notes

'The chief person of our little community (commonly called the *Governor*) is Mr. Glass' (Earle, *Journal* [1966], p.207. He is shown leaning against a fence in front of his cottage (known as 'Government House'). A Scotsman from Kelso in Roxburghshire, Glass enlisted in the army and was sent to the Cape Colony. In 1816 he formed part of a garrison attached to Tristan da Cunha, sent to prevent the island being

used as a base for any attempt to rescue Napoleon from St Helena. When the garrison was withdrawn in 1817, Glass requested permission to remain. He died on Tristan da Cunha on 24 November 1853.

Earle exhibited a similar watercolour in October 1826 at his gallery in Sydney, entitled 'Government House at Tristan D'Acunha'. This painting is described by the Reverend John McGarvie in his diary entry for 27 October 1826 and in the *Sydney Gazette* of 30 July 1829. It seems that Glass was not included in this version of the subject.

39 Solitude, — Tristan D'Acunha, — Watching the horizon (1824) (NK 12/3)

Inscription	'3. Solitude, — Watching the horizon at Sun Set, in the hopes of seeing a Vessel, — Tristan De Acunha, in the South Atlantic' on mount
Reverse	'Solitude watching the horizon at Sunset in hopes of seeing a Vessel Tristan de Acunha' Attached to two sheets of backing paper with pencil sketches. The first sketch shows moving horses with attendants wearing turbans The second sketch is of a ladder or stairway
Watercolour	17.5 x 25.7 cm
Exhibited	Rex Nan Kivell Collection Exhibition. NLA, 1974

Notes

A watercolour entitled 'Solitude' was exhibited by Earle in June 1826 at his gallery and is mentioned in McGarvie's diary for 27 October 1826. However the ideal and 'serene' scenery described in the *Sydney Gazette* of 30 July 1829 suggests a different painting.

40 Squall, off Tristan D'Acunha (1824) (NK 12/4)

Inscription	'4. Squall off Tristan D'Acunha' on mount
Reverse	Faint pencil outline of a mountain. 'Dark cloud' (l.l.), 'Ruddah' [?] (u.l.), 'W.S.W.' (u.c.) Attached to three sheets of backing paper, two of which have been taken from a naval reference book. The third is from a log-book
Watercolour	17.5 x 25.7 cm

Notes

In his journal Earle frequently described these violent squalls, christened 'Willies' by the islanders. Together with the heavy surf and treacherous rocks, they were responsible for the many shipwrecks occurring in the area.

41 Tristan D'Acunha (1824) (NK 12/5)
Inscription   '5. Tristan D'Acunha' on
                 mount
Reverse   'Tristan de Acunha'
Watercolour   17.1 x 25.7 cm
Exhibited   Rex Nan Kivell Collection
                 Exhibition. NLA, 1974
Notes
   Although the island covers 104 square

km, most of this area is uninhabitable.
The village was situated at the foot of
steep mountains, on a strip of fertile land
sloping down towards the sea, 'but it is
cut suddenly from the beach by an abrupt
precipice of about fifty feet' (Earle,
Journal [1966], p.220). Here also were
cultivated the potatoes for which Tristan
da Cunha is famed.

   The two women pictured (the only
women residents on the island) are Mrs
Glass and Mrs White. Mrs Glass was a
Cape Creole who married Glass in 1814.
Mrs White, a half-caste Portuguese,
married Stephen White in 1821 at Tristan
da Cunha. They were both survivors from
the *Blenden Hall*, wrecked on a
neighbouring island in 1821.

42 Governor Glass & his Companions, Tristan D'Acunha (1824) (NK 12/6)

Inscription   '6. Governor Glass and Companions, Tristan D'Acunha' on mount

Reverse   'Governor Glass and companions on Tristan de Acunha the Gov.r is lighting his pipe'

Watercolour   17.5 x 26 cm

Exhibited   Rex Nan Kivell Collection Exhibition. NLA, 1974

Notes

The eight adult inhabitants of the island are pictured around the table at 'Government House'. As well as Earle and Gooch, there are the four residents previously described, the Glass and White couples, and two other permanent residents, John Taylor and Richard Riley. Riley, an ex-sailor, fisherman and cook known as 'Old Dick', was shipwrecked on the island and remained, 'preferring the sort of life led here' (Earle, *Journal* [1966], p.217). Earle is seated (l.r.) with his back to the spectator, and a dog lying at his feet. Mrs Glass is standing at the doorway, while her husband (as described by Earle on the reverse of the painting) is the figure standing lighting his pipe.

On the wall (t.l.) behind the door there seems to be a framed proclamation — perhaps the letter from the army mentioned in the journal, approving Glass's discharge from service, and permitting him to remain on the island.

In his diary for 27 October 1826, McGarvie mentions a painting entitled 'Governor Glass and associates at Dinner — Portraits'.

43 Tristan D'Acunha (1824) (NK 12/7)
Inscription   '7. Tristan D'Acunha' on
                  mount
Reverse   'Tristan de Acunha'
Watercolour   17.5 x 26 cm
Notes

   View painted from the top near Little
Beach, looking south-southeast. The pole
(l.r.) marked 'the spot where the remains
of the unhappy sufferers were interred'
(Earle, *Journal* [1966], p.210). Earle is
referring to the crew of the *Julia*, wrecked
in October 1817. He pointed out, 'The
wreck has been of great service to the
inhabitants; for their houses and fences
are principally composed of it' (Earle,
Journal [1966], p.210).
In the foreground (l.c.) is the artist with
a dog.

44 Tristan D'Acunha (1824) (NK 12/8)
Inscription   '8. Tristan D'Acunha' on
                  mount
Reverse   'Tristan de Acunha'
Watercolour   17.1 x 25.7 cm
Notes

   Earle is pictured in the foreground,
with a dog.

45 Flinching a young Sea Elephant
(1824) (NK 12/9)

Inscription   '9. Flinching a Yearling, a
               young Sea Elephant,
               Tristan D'Acunha' on
               mount
Reverse   'Flinching a (yearling) or
               young Sea Elephant.
               Tristan de Acunha'
Watercolour   17.5 x 26 cm
Notes

In his journal Earle described the
hunting of sea elephants, valued by the
islanders for their blubber and skins. The
hide of the bull-elephant was used for
shoe leather, while the softer fur of the
pups was made into caps.

A watercolour entitled 'Killing Sea
Elephants' was exhibited by Earle in June
1826 in Sydney and depicted a man in the
act of killing a sea elephant (see Sydney
Gazette, 30 July 1829). It may have been
a companion piece to this illustration.

46 Nightingale Island near Tristan
D'Acunha (1824) (NK 12/10)
Inscription   '10. Nightingale Island,
               near Tristan D'Acunha,
               with my little Vessel The
               Duke of Gloucester,

Reverse   Margate Hoy' on mount
               'Nightingale Island near
               Tristan de Acunha with
               my little vessel the Duke
               of Gloucester Margate
               Hoy'
Watercolour   14 x 25.7 cm.

The painting is attached to
two sheets of paper, one of
which has been taken from
a log-book. The second is a
handwritten navigational
exercise

47 Rafting Blubber at Tristan D'Acunha

(1824) (NK 12/11)

Inscription	'11. Rafting Blubber at Tristan D'Acunha, a Companion to Killing Sea Elephants' on mount Illegible writing — colour note? (t.r.)
Watercolour	21.6 x 34.9 cm Paper scratched to indicate highlights in surf
Exhibited	Rex Nan Kivell Collection Exhibition. NLA, 1974

Notes

Earle is pictured sitting with a dog (l.r.). H. E. Spencer, in *Augustus Earle*, p.423, notes that the number of men pictured in the whaleboat exceeded by one the adult male population of the island at the time of Earle's stay there. In the foreground, a sailor on the shore is guiding slabs of blubber strung on a rope through the surf towards a whaleboat. 'This valuable article, my comrades, with incredible labour, difficulty, and some danger, got into their boat; and the skill and address used in getting off the beach in such a situation, and through such a strong surf, proves what men can accomplish . . .' (Earle, *Journal* [1966], p.233). The boat then returned with the blubber to the settlement on the other side of the island.

48 A North Easter, Tristan D'Acunha

(1824) (NK 12/13)

Inscription	'13. A North Easter, Tristan D'Acunha' on mount
Reverse	Painting attached to a page from a log-book. Letters of the alphabet have been transcribed over the log-book entries
Watercolour	19 x 33 cm Narrow horizontal strip added to the upper and lower edge of the painting

Notes

In his journal, Earle noted the effects of these northeasters: 'The sea breaks with violence over rocks which are just rising above water, and the whole extent of beach is whitened with surf.' (Earle, *Journal* [1966], p.205). The figure in the foreground (l.r.) is probably the artist.

49 View on the Summit at Tristan D'Acunha (1824) (NK 12/14)

Inscription   '14. View on the Summit at Tristan D'Acunha 1824' on mount

Watercolour 20 x 33.5 cm

Notes

The view is probably of Green Hill, or one of the high under-cones below the extinct volcano, which rises to a peak of 2060 m.

On 28 May 1824, Earle 'accompanied by two of the men . . . determined to ascend the mountain . . . we gained the summit, where we found ourselves on an extended plain, of several miles' expanse, which terminates in the peak, composed of dark grey lava, bare and frightful to behold' (Earle, *Journal* [1966], p.222). 'The object of my comrades . . . was neither to procure the feathers of the albatross, nor to admire the sublime scenery. Goats, of which there are thousands on these plains, were the ostensible cause of their coming' (Earle, *Journal* [1966], p.222). Earle is seen in the foreground, while one of his companions may be seen further back (t.l.), giving chase to a herd of goats.

50 A man killing Albatross Tristan D'Acunha (1824) (NK 12/15)

Inscription   '15. Summit of Tristan D'Acunha, a man killing Albatross' on mount

Watercolour 19.3 x 33.3 cm

Notes

During the same expedition (*see* Notes, no. 49) Earle and his friends encountered some albatross. 'The old ones, which are valuable on account of their feathers, my companions made dreadful havoc amongst, knocking on the head all they could come up with' (Earle, *Journal* [1966], p.223).

51 Tristan D'Acunha (1824) (NK 12/16)

Inscription   '16. Tristan D'Acunha' on
                  mount
                  L. to r. 'Dark', 'light',
                  'green' (?), 'mountains' (?)

Reverse   'Tristan da Acunha'

Watercolour   25.4 x 17.1 cm

Notes

   Earle is pictured with a dog (l.r.),
resting on a rock in the course of one of
his daily quests for food to help
supplement the basic diet of milk and
potatoes. Behind him lies the precipitous
Tristan da Cunha mountain range.

52 Tristan D'Acunha (1824) (NK 12/17)

Inscription   '17. Tristan D'Acunha' on
                  mount

Reverse   'Tristan de Acunha'

Watercolour   25.7 x 17.1 cm.

53 My Dog Jemmy (c. 1824) (NK 12/58)
Inscription   '58. My Dog Jemmy' on
                mount
Watercolour   10.2 x 14.6 cm
Notes
    Jemmy spent eight months with Earle
as a castaway on Tristan da Cunha.

**54 Scudding before a heavy Gale off the
Cape, Lat. 44°** (1824) (NK 12/128)
Inscription   '128. Scudding before a
                heavy Westerley Gale off
                the Cape; — Latitude 44°'
                on mount
Reverse   'Scudding before a heavy
                Westerly gale off the Cape
                Latitude 44°'
Watercolour   20.6 x 27.3 cm
Exhibited   Rex Nan Kivell Collection
                Exhibition. NLA, 1974
Notes
    H.E. Spencer in *Augustus Earle*, p.425-
6, has established that the scene took
place on the *Admiral Cockburn*, sailing
between Tristan da Cunha and Van
Diemen's Land in November 1824. The
latitude given must refer to the Cape of
Good Hope, with the vessel running
before the westerly gales. This was the
only time in his travels that Earle was in
this position and taking this course. The
man seated dozing (l.l.) is most probably
the artist, with Jemmy at his feet.

55 Speaking a Vessel off the Cape of Good Hope (1824) (NK 12/129)

Inscription   '129. Speaking a Vessel off
               the Cape of Good Hope'
               on mount
Reverse   'Speaking a Vessel off the
               Cape of Good Hope' in ink
Watercolour   21 x 27.3 cm
Exhibited   Rex Nan Kivell Collection
               Exhibition. NLA, 1974

Notes

The similarities with no. 54 indicate that the painting dates from the same voyage. H.E. Spencer, *Augustus Earle*, p.425, noted that the *Australian* recorded on 27 January 1825 a meeting between the *Admiral Cockburn* and the *Grenada*. 'The ships remained together during the night with the intention of communicating by boats in the morning; but the weather being too rough, sail was again made.' This may be a contemporary description of the scene described in the watercolour. Further, the costume of the men and the lady suggest the early 1820s rather than c.1830 (the only other time Earle rounded the Cape). The two paintings, therefore, must date from this 1824 period.

56 Cape Barathus Adventure Bay V.D. Land (1825) (NK 12/20)

Inscription   'Cape Barathas [Barathus]
               Adventure Bay Van
               Dieman's Land' on mount
Reverse   'Cape Barathus Adventure
               Bay. V.D. Land'
Watercolour   17.5 x 26.3 cm

Notes

Cape Barathus is on the south coast of Tasmania, 48 km south of Hobart.

58 The Coast of New Holland, New South Wales (1825) (NK 12/19)

Inscription   '19. Coast of New Holland, New South Wales' on mount
Reverse   'Coast of New Holland'
Watercolour   17.1 x 25.7 cm

57 June Park, Van Dieman's Land, perfect Park Scenery (1825) (NK 12/27)

Inscription   '27. June Park Van Dieman's Land, the grand appearance of the Country in its natural state, Perfect Park Scenery' on mount
Reverse   'Clune Park. V.D. Land. The general appearance of the country in its natural state, perfect Park scenery'
Watercolour   24.2 x 40.3 cm
Exhibited   Rex Nan Kivell Collection Exhibition. NLA, 1974

Notes

Earle has written the title as 'Clune Park' on the reverse of the painting. The title on the mount (written in another hand) refers to June Park; hence the confusion. It would appear that Clune Park is the correct title. Earle is probably thinking of Cluny Park, of Bark Hut Plains which is 90 km northwest of Hobart. Earle may have spent some time there during his eight months' residence in Van Diemen's Land.

59 South Head & Light House. Port Jackson N.S. Wales (c. 1825) (NK 12/21)

Inscription   '21. South Hea ¹ and Light House, Port Ja kson, N.S. Wales, with the approach of a Southerly Squall' on mount

Watercolour   10.8 x 34.9 cm
Two sheets joined at centre

Notes

In both the *Sydney Gazette* of 30 July 1829 and in his diary for 27 October 1826, the Rev. John McGarvie described the pictures in Earle's gallery, which he visited on 27 October 1826. He mentioned a 'View of Macquarie Light house on the South Head of Port Jackson. This . . . very interesting object, seen thirty miles at sea by every ship entering the port . . . . As this is the most southernly lighthouse in the world, it

derives an importance from that circumstance . . . . '(*Sydney Gazette*, 30 July 1829). The lighthouse was the first to be constructed in Australia and was built in 1817. The architect was Francis Greenway. In 1883 it was replaced by the present South Head Lighthouse.

There is a similar lithographic print of the lighthouse and South Head in Earle's *Views in Australia,* printed by the artist in Sydney in 1826.

60 Port Jackson, New South Wales (c. 1825) (NK 12/22)

Inscription   '22. Port Jackson New South Wales' on mount

Watercolour   10.8 x 35.2 cm
Two sheets joined at centre.

61 Port Jackson, New South Wales
(c. 1825) (NK 12/25)

Inscription	'25. Port Jackson' on mount
Reverse	'Port Jackson'
Watercolour	22.5 x 32.4 cm Horizontal section added, top.

62 Remarkable Passage in the Cliffs Port Jackson (c. 1825) (NK 12/62)

Inscription	'62. Remarkable Passage down the Cliffs south head Port Jackson' on mount
Watercolour	25.4 x 11.4 cm Upper section joined to painting.

63 View from the Summit of the South Head near Sidney [sic] (c. 1825)
(NK 12/36)

Inscription	'36. Near Sidney from the Summit of the South Head close to the Light House, used as a Black Smith's Shop. N.S. Wales' on mount
Reverse	'Near Sidney, from the summit of the S. Head close to the lighthouse used as a black smith's shop, N.S. Wales'
Watercolour	22.2 x 31.1 cm.

64 South Head Light. N.S. Wales
(c. 1825) (NK 12/59)

Inscription	'59. South Head Light New South Wales' on mount
Reverse	'South Head Cliffs N.S.W.'
Watercolour	10.8 x 16.5 cm
Notes	*See* Notes, no. 59.

65 The Head of a Gentleman, a Portrait

(c. 1825) (NK 12/164)
No inscription '164' on mount
Watercolour   14.6 x 14 cm
Notes
   Collar and shoulders sketched in pencil.
H.E. Spencer, 'The Brisbane Portraits',
*Journal of the Royal Australian Historical
Society* 52 (March 1966): 1-9, identified
it as a preliminary sketch for the large oil
portrait of Sir Thomas Brisbane in
Government House, Sydney.
   The Reverend John McGarvie also
mentioned a small watercolour sketch of
the Governor exhibited at Earle's gallery
in July 1826 (*see* McGarvie's diary and
Sydney Gazette for 30 July 1829).

66 A Native Camp of Australian Savages

(1826) (NK 12/28)
Inscription   '28. A Native Camp of
                 Australian Savages near
                 Port Stevens, New South
                 Wales' on mount
Reverse   'A Native Camp of
                 Australian Savages, near
                 Port Stevens. N.S.W.'
Watercolour   25.1 x 43.8 cm
Exhibited   Rex Nan Kivell Collection
                 Exhibition. NLA, 1974
Notes
   Earle visited the Hunter River, Port
Stephens and Port Macquarie late in
1826.

67 On The Hunter River, N.S. Wales
(1826) (NK 12/29)

Inscription	'29. Hunter's River, New South Wales, 1826' on mount
	L. to r. 'Birds' (l.r.)
Watercolour	22.5 x 29.2 cm
Notes	*See* Notes, no. 66.

**68 Female Orphan School, Paramatta
N.S. Wales** (1825-7) (NK 12/30)

Inscription	'30. Female Orphan School, Parramatta, N.S. Wales' on mount
Watercolour	17.8 x 30.8 cm
Exhibited	Australian and Pacific material from the Nan Kivell Collection. Adelaide Festival of Arts, March 1962

Notes

Work on the school began in 1801 but the building was not completed until 1818. The Rev. Samuel Marsden supervised its construction and management. The building still stands as part of the Rydalmere Mental Hospital. Joseph Lycett also published in 1825 a coloured aquatint entitled 'View of the Female Orphan School', a frontal view of the orphanage, seen from across the Parramatta River.

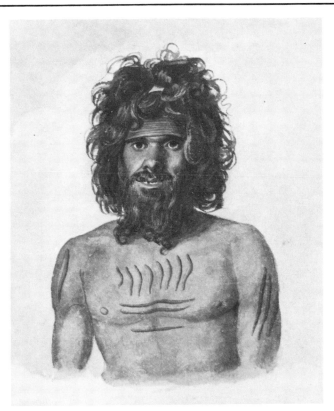

69 A Man of New South Wales (1825-7)
(NK 12/34)
Inscription   '34. A Man of New South
              Wales' on mount
Watercolour   24.8 x 18.7 cm

70 A Woman of New South Wales
(1825-7) (NK 12/35)
Inscription   '35. A Woman of New
              South Wales' on mount
Watercolour   24.8 x 18.7 cm
Notes
  The darker spots visible on the
woman's body are due to the subsequent
retouching of mould areas, which later
absorbed the new pigment.

71 A Female Penitentiary, Paramatta N.S. Wales (1825-7) (NK 12/47)

Inscription '47. Female Penitentiary, or Factory, Parramata [sic], N.S. Wales' on mount

Watercolour 15.9 x 25.7 cm

Exhibited Australian and Pacific material from the Nan Kivell Collection. Adelaide Festival of Arts, March 1962

Notes

Convict women not assigned as domestic servants upon arrival in the colony were sent to the Female Factory at Parramatta. Completed in 1821, the building was designed by Francis Greenway. The Rev. Samuel Marsden also supervised its planning.

72 An Australian Native in his Bark Hut (c. 1825-7) (NK 12/52)

Inscription '52. Australian Native in his Bark Hut' on mount

Reverse 'Australian Native in his Bark Hut'

Watercolour 18.1 x 19.4 cm

73 Point Piper near Sidney New South Wales (c. 1826) (NK 12/53)

Inscription	'53. Point Piper near Sydney N.S. Wales' on mount
Reverse	'Point Piper near Sydney N.S. Wales'
Watercolour	15.5 x 20.6 cm

Notes

A similar view is reproduced in lithographic form in Earle's *Views in New South Wales and Van Diemen's Land* (Part I, plate 2). In the accompanying description, Earle noted that 'the first pleasing object which breaks suddenly on the sight after having entered the Port, is Point Piper; so called from a worthy Gentleman of that name chusing this spot for his residence'. The house in the foreground, 'Henrietta Villa', was built by Captain Piper in 1816 and appears also in a pen and ink sketch, *Point Piper, New South Wales* (no. 80) as well as in the background of Earle's oil portrait of *Captain John Piper* (ML 6, Gallery).

74 A Native Man, Australia (c. 1826) (NK 12/54)

Inscription	'54. Native Man, Australia' on mount
Watercolour	16.5 x 17.5 cm.

75 A Native Woman, Australia
(c. 1825-7) (NK 12/55)
Inscription   '55. Native Woman, —
                 Australia' on mount
Watercolour   15.9 x 17.5 cm.

**76 Annual Meeting of Native Tribes at
Paramatta** (c. 1825-7) (NK 12/57)
Inscription   '57. The Annual Meeting
                 of the Native Tribes at
                 Parramatta New South
                 Wales. — The Governor
                 meeting them' on mount
                 'H.I.' (l.r.)
Reverse   'The annual meeting of
                 the native tribes at
                 Parramatta
                 The Govr visiting them'
Watercolour   17.1 x 26 cm
Exhibited   Rex Nan Kivell Collection
                 Exhibition. NLA, 1974
Notes
   A conservation report suggests that
this painting was originally much
brighter and has faded considerably since
execution. On Saturday 28 December
1816, Governor Macquarie invited the
natives to a friendly meeting in the
market place at Parramatta, at which he
confirmed the rank of the Aboriginal
chiefs. The natives formed a circle with
the chiefs seated on chairs, the
remainder on the ground. 'Large tables
groaning under the weight of roast beef,
potatoes, bread, &c. and a large cask of
grog lent its exhilarating aid to promote
the general festivity . . .'
(*Sydney Gazette*, 4 January 1817). By
the end of the following decade these
meetings had died out. (For further
comments on this painting, *see*
Introduction).

77 Desmond, A New South Wales Chief
(c. 1825-7) (NK 12/61)

Inscription	'61. Desmond, a N.S. Wales Chief painted for a Rarobb [corroboree] or Native Dance' on mount
Watercolour	25.7 x 17.5 cm Lower section joined to painting
Exhibited	Australian Painting, XIX and XX Century. Auckland, 1964. Exhibition assembled by the Commonwealth Arts Advisory Board.

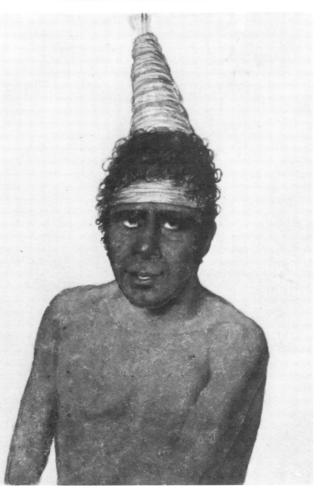

78 A Native Man. N.S. Wales (1825)
(NK 12/63)

No inscription	See no. 79. 'Tommy' (t.r.), 'Newcastle. 1825' Horizontal strip of paper inscribed with the number '63' in pencil added to lower edge
Watercolour	21 x 15.9 cm
Notes	

In the inscription to no. 79, Earle indicated that this painting of an Aboriginal was done around the Newcastle region, north of Sydney.

79 A Native Woman. N.S. Wales
(c. 1825) (NK 12/64)
Inscription   '63. & 64. Natives of New
                 South Wales' on mount
Watercolour   19.8 x 16 cm
Notes
    As the inscription on this painting is
linked with that of no. 78, it is reasonable
to assume that this native woman was
also from the Newcastle district.

80 Point Piper, New South Wales
(c. 1826) (NK 12/149)
Inscription   '149. Point Piper New
                 South Wales' on mount
                 'Point Piper' (l.r.) in ink
Pen and ink   18.4 x 26.4 cm
Notes   *See* Notes, no. 73. Captain
                 Piper's house 'Henrietta
                 Villa' is visible (u.c.), with
                 a view of Point Piper and
                 Sydney Harbour in the
                 background.

81 The Norfolk Pine, New South Wales

(c. 1825-7) (NK 12/152)

Inscription '152. The Norfolk Pine
N.S. Wales' on mount
'The Norfolk Pine, this is
a study of one of those
trees at the entrance of the
Government domain, near
the gate w[h]ere the
Governor is seen entering,
however, they may vary in
height. The leaves are all
the same size' in ink

Watercolour 17.3 x 10.5 cm.

82 View from the Summit of Mount York, N.S. Wales (c. 1826-7) (NK 12/23)

Inscription '23. View from the Summit
of Mount York, looking
towards Bathurst Plains,
Convicts breaking Stones,
N.S. Wales' on mount
Narrow strip (with title)
added along bottom edge

Watercolour 22.5 x 33 cm
Exhibited Rex Nan Kivell Collection
Exhibition. NLA, 1974
Australian Painting, XIX
and XX Century.
Auckland, 1964.
Exhibition assembled by
the Commonwealth Arts
Advisory Board

Notes
'The delinquents are employed in
forming new roads, by cutting through
mountains, blasting rocks . . . .' (H.W.D.,
*State of Convicts in New South Wales,
1835*). Earle visited the Blue Mountains,
Bathurst and the Wellington Valley in
1826.

83 Wellington Valley, N.S. Wales
(c. 1826-7) (NK 12/24)

Inscription	'24. Wellington Valley, New South Wales, looking East, from Government House' on mount l. to r. 'brown', 'light green', 'green', 'straw' [?]
Reverse	'Wellington Valley N.S. Wales looking E. from Government House'
Watercolour	20 x 37.5 cm
Exhibited	Rex Nan Kivell Collection Exhibition. NLA, 1974

Notes

A convict settlement was established at Wellington Valley in 1823, and it is likely that Earle was referring to the Commandant's house when he wrote 'Government House'.

84 Kings Table Land, Blue Mountains, N.S. Wales (c. 1826-7) (NK 12/26)

Inscription	'26. King's Table Land, Bleu Mountains, New South Wales, the appearance of the New Road' on mount
Reverse	'King's Table Land, Blue Mountains N.S. Wales. The appearance of the New Road'
Watercolour	21.3 x 36.2 cm Scratches in pigment to indicate light and atmosphere
Exhibited	Rex Nan Kivell Collection Exhibition. NLA, 1974.

85 Native of N.S. Wales Wellington Valley (c. 1826-7) (NK 12/32)

No inscription *See* no. 86. Horizontal strip of paper added along the lower edge inscribed with the number '32'

Reverse   'Native of New South Wales'
Watercolour 24.1 x 18.4 cm
Exhibited   Rex Nan Kivell Collection Exhibition. NLA, 1974

Notes

Early in 1826, Earle made a trip to Emu Plains, the Blue Mountains, Bathurst and Wellington Valley. Discovered by Oxley in 1817, Wellington Valley is situated at the junction of the Bell and Macquarie rivers, 380 km northwest of Sydney and 188 km northwest of Bathurst.

Cicatrisation marks may be seen on the Aboriginal's back. This process is still practised today. A sharp piece of flint was used to incise the skin, and clay and ashes were then rubbed into the wound to prevent it healing properly, resulting in a series of upraised scars on the body. Nos 69, 70 and 86 also show evidence of cicatrisation.

86 Native of Wellington Valley (c. 1826-7) (NK 12/33)

Inscription '32. & 33. Natives of New South Wales from Wellington Valley' on mount
Reverse   Horizontal strip of paper added to lower edge inscribed with the title 'Native of N.S. Wales, from Wellington Valley'
Watercolour 23.8 x 19 cm
Exhibited   Rex Nan Kivell Collection Exhibition. NLA, 1974.

**87 Mosmans Cave, Wellington Valley,
N.S. Wales No. 1** (c. 1826-7) (NK 12/41)

Inscription	'41. Mosman's Cave, Wellington Valley New South Wales, No. 1' on mount
Reverse	'Mosman's Cave, Wellington Valley'
Watercolour	21 x 32.4 cm

Notes
Wellington Valley was famed for its limestone caves.

**88 Mosmans Cave, Wellington Valley,
N.S. Wales No. 5** (c. 1826-7) (NK 12/42)

Inscription	'42. Mosman's Cave Wellington Valley N.S. Wales No. 5' on mount
Watercolour	13.3 x 10.8 cm

Notes
The sectional drawing shows a series of underground caves with extensive stalactite and stalagmite formations.

89 Mosmans Cave, Wellington Valley, N.S. Wales No. 3 (c. 1826-7) (NK 12/43)

Inscription	'43. Mosman's Cave, Wellington Valley, New South Wales No. 3' on mount
Reverse	'Mosman's Cave N.S.W.'
Watercolour	34 x 22.9 cm.

90 A Native Family of N.S. Wales (c. 1826-7) (NK 12/45)

Inscription	'45. A Native Family of New South Wales sitting down on an English Settlers Farm' on mount Indistinguishable writing (l.l.)
Watercolour	17.5 x 25.7 cm
Notes	

The woman (left) bears a resemblance to one of Bungaree's wives, portrayed in Earle's *Views in New South Wales and Van Diemen's Land* (Part 2, plate 1), but appears slightly younger than the woman in the lithograph.

**91 The Farm House of W. Lawson Esq.
N.S. Wales** (c. 1826-7) (NK 12/51)

Inscription   '51. The Farm House of
                   W. Lawson Esqre. N.S.
                   Wales' on mount
Watercolour   12.7 x 25.7 cm
Exhibited   Rex Nan Kivell Collection
                   Exhibition. NLA, 1974

Notes

   In both the *Sydney Gazette* (30 July
1829) and his diary entry for 27 October
1826, McGarvie described a variant of
this painting, which depicted Mr Lawson
in a landscape setting. Lawson's farm
was at Prospect Hill, between
Parramatta and Penrith.

**92 The Blue Mountains from the Emu
Plains' road** (c. 1826-7) (NK 12/56)

Inscription   '56. A distant View of
                   the Blue Mountains and
                   Lapston Hill, New South
                   Wales, taken from the
                   Emu Plains Road' on
                   mount
Watercolour   10.8 x 17.8 cm.

93 Cabbage Tree Forest, Ilawarra, New South Wales (1827) (NK 12/37)

Inscription   '37. Cabbage Tree Forest, Illawarra New South Wales' on mount
Narrow horizontal strip of paper inscribed with title added to lower edge

Watercolour   25.7 x 17.1 cm.

Notes

In April-May 1827, Earle made a sketching trip to the Illawarra (or Five Islands) district. This area is about 100 km south of Sydney, extending from the coast to the Illawarra and Cambewarra ranges. Inland, the scenery varies from the farmlands of the coastal plain (*see* nos 97-9) to more rugged mountainous country and rain forest (nos 87, 93-6 and 100). It was accessible by both land and sea, a land route having been discovered by Charles Throsby in 1815.

94 Cabbage Tree Forest, Ilawarra, New South Wales (1827) (NK 12/38)

No inscription Horizontal strip of paper inscribed with the number '38' added to lower edge

Watercolour   25.7 x 17.1 cm.

95 A Bivouack, day break, on the Ilawarra Mountains (1827) (NK 12/39)

Inscription   '39. & 40. A Bivouack in
                   New South Wales, Day
                   breaking' on mount
                   Horizontal strip of paper
                   inscribed with the title
                   added to lower edge
Watercolour   25.7 x 17.5 cm
Exhibited   Australian Painting, XIX
                   and XX Century.
                   Auckland, 1964.
                   Exhibition assembled by
                   the Commonwealth Arts
                   Advisory Board.

96 A Bivouack, day break, on the Ilawarra Mountains (1827) (NK 12/40)

Inscription   'The Hollow Tree on the
                   Illawarra Mountains, New
                   South Wales' on mount
                   Horizontal strip of paper
                   inscribed with the title
                   added to lower edge
                   Numbered in pencil in l.l.
                   corner in unknown hand
Watercolour   26 x 17.5 cm
Exhibited   Rex Nan Kivell Collection
                   Exhibition. NLA, 1974.

97 Mr Cowells Farm on the Coast 60 miles South of Sidney [sic] (1827)
(NK 12/44)

Inscription	'44. Mr Cowell's Farm on the Coast, 60 miles South of Sidney' on mount
Reverse	'Mr Cowell's Farm, on the Coast 60 miles south of Sydney'
Watercolour	15.6 x 25.7 cm
Exhibited	Rex Nan Kivell Collection Exhibition. NLA, 1974

Notes

Landward exploitation and settlement of the coastal areas in the Illawarra district began in 1816.

98 View on the Coast of N.S. Wales Ilawarra (1827) (NK 12/46)

Inscription	'46. View on the Coast of New South Wales — Illawarra' on mount
Reverse	'View on the Coast of New South Wales'
Watercolour	17.5 x 25.7 cm

Notes

In the *Sydney Gazette* of 30 July 1829, McGarvie described this 'ideal view of a huge perforated rock', which he had seen at Earle's exhibition in June 1826. Today it is better known as the blow-hole at Kiama.

The rather theatrical contrast of the dark cavernous interior with the clear sky beyond is similar to the earlier maquette for the pantomime 'The Wonders of Derbyshire' (1778) by Philippe Jacques de Loutherbourg, a French artist who worked as a stage designer in London. It also resembles Joseph Wright's dramatic and romantic scene of Ferdinand and Miranda in *Prospero's Cell* which Earle may have seen after it was reproduced as an engraving.

**99 Ilawarra, Scene on the Coast of N.S.
Wales** (1827) (NK 12/48)
Inscription   '48. Scene on the Coast of
                 New South Wales —
                 Illawarra' on mount
Watercolour   17.1 x 26 cm.

**100 Skirmish, Bush Rangers &
Constables, Ilawarra** (1827) (NK 12/49)
Inscription   '49. Skirmish between
                 Bushrangers and
                 Constables, Illawarra' on
                 mount
Watercolour   17.5 x 26 cm
                 Scratches in paint to
                 indicate highlights in
                 water.

101 Curious Rocks & Natural Baths N.S. Wales (1827) (NK 12/50)

Inscription   '50. Curious Rocks, and Natural Baths, New South Wales' on mount

Watercolour   17.8 x 26.3 cm

Notes
   This view was probably also painted on the south coast of New South Wales near the Illawarra.

102 The Emu, N.S. Wales (1827) (NK 12/60)

Inscription   '60. Emu, New South Wales, 1827' on mount

Watercolour   12.7 x 14.9 cm
               Horizontal strip attached to lower section of painting.

103 The Cabbage Tree New South Wales
(1827) (NK 12/153)
Inscription   '153. The Cabbage Tree
                 New South Wales' on
                 mount
                 'Cabbage Tree, N.S.
                 Wales' (l.r.) [pencil on
                 painting]
Watercolour   26.1 x 17.5 cm.

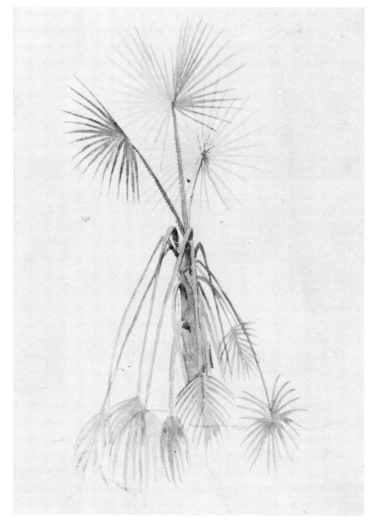

104 Entrance of the E O Ke Angha New Zealand [Hokianga] (1827) (NK 12/136)
Inscription   '136. New Zealand, The
                 Entrance of the E.O.K.
                 Angha River; View taken
                 from the Bar' on mount
Watercolour   14 x 58.7 cm
                 Two sheets joined at the
                 centre
Exhibited   The Rex Nan Kivell
                 Exhibition of Early New
                 Zealand Pictures.

Alexander Turnbull
Library, Wellington, 1953
Early Watercolours of
New Zealand. Auckland
City Art Gallery, 1963

Notes
    This was probably Earle's first study
of New Zealand. 'The entrance to this
river is very remarkable, and can never
be mistaken by mariners. On the north
side, for many miles, are hills of sand,
white, bleak, and barren, ending

abruptly at the entrance of the river,
which is about a quarter of a mile across.
Where the south head rises abrupt,
craggy, and black, . . . thus at the first
glimpse of these heads from the sea, one
is white, the other black . . . the bar . . .
lies two miles from the mouth of the
river, its head enveloped in breakers and
foam . . . .' (Earle, *Narrative* [1966], p.56).
See also Notes, no. 105.

105 Entrance of the E.O. Ke Angha River (1827) (NK 12/67)

Inscription
'67. View of the Village of Parcuncigh and the Entrance of the E-O-Ke-Angha River, New Zealand' on mount l. to r. 'sand' [?], 'sand', illegible word, 'Dark', 'Village of Parcuncigh E.O. Keangha . . . [?] Zealand'
Horizontal strip of paper inscribed with title added to lower edge

Watercolour 24.4 x 44.4 cm

Notes

Earle arrived in New Zealand on 31 October 1827, on board the *Governor Macquarie*. After successfully crossing the extremely treacherous bar at the head of the Hokianga River, the brig sailed into the Hokianga Harbour (on the west coast of the North Island) and cast anchor at the village of Pakanae.

'On November 3d we visited Par Finneigh [Pakanae], a village lying round the base of a large conical hill, about three hundred feet high, with a fortification on the top, which gives it its name, Par [pa] signifying in their language, a fortified place.' (Earle, *Narrative* [1966], p.62). 'The village . . . is, in fact, a collection of rude huts, huddled together without system or regularity . . . few being more than four feet high, with a door-way about two feet.' (Earle, *Narrative* [1966], p.62). Behind the village was a swamp. 'To the right of this swamp is a beautiful valley . . . . At the time I stood viewing it from the summit of the hill, I was charmed with the scene of industry and bustle it presented; all the inhabitants of the village having gone forth to plant their potatoes, kumeras, and Indian corn. In the rear . . . is an immense chain of high and rugged hills, covered to their summits with thick forests . . . .' (Earle, *Narrative* [1966], p.62).

106 A Fortified Island in the E.O. Ke
Angha River (1827) (NK 12/68)
Inscription   '68. A Fortified Island in
               E-O-Ke-Angha River New
               Zealand'
               Horizontal strip of paper
               inscribed with title added
               to lower edge
Watercolour   18.7 x 33.7 cm
Exhibited   The Rex Nan Kivell
               Exhibition of Early New
               Zealand Pictures

Alexander Turnbull
Library, Wellington, 1953
Early Watercolours of
New Zealand. Auckland
City Art Gallery, 1963

Notes
    The island of Motiti is situated in
Hokianga Harbour approximately 20
kilometres northeast of Pakanae. The
Governor Macquarie went aground just
opposite the island (l.r.) 'and had to
remain there till the next tide floated her

off. It was a curious and interesting spot,
being a native par and depôt, and was
entirely covered with storehouses for
provisions and ammunition. The centre
was so contrived that all assailants
might be cut off before they could effect
a landing; and we were all much
gratified by the judgment and
forethought displayed in this little
military work.' (Earle, *Narrative* [1966],
p.66).

107 Dock Yard in the Shu Keangha
River New Zealand (1827) (NK 12/137)
Inscription   '137. The Showrackki,
               commonly called Deptford
               Dock Yard, a Ship-
               building Establishment
               belonging to some Sydney
               Merchants in the
               Shukeangha River New
               Zealand. —' on mount
               l. to r. 'heath' [?], 'light',
               'woods', 'light green',
               'woods', 'stumps on [?]
               the land' (l.r.) in ink
Watercolour   17.1 x 51.4 cm
               Two sheets joined
               together at centre
Exhibited   Early Watercolours of
               New Zealand. Auckland
               City Art Gallery, 1963

Notes
    Deptford Dockyard is situated a few
kilometres northwest of Pakanae, in
Hokianga Harbour. The shipyard was
owned by three Sydney merchants,
Raine, Ramsay and Gordon Browne, who
established the dockyard and sawpits. It
was managed at the time of Earle's visit
by Captain David Clark.
    'Several vessels have been laden with
timber and spars; one vessel has been
built, launched, and sent to sea from this
spot; and another of a hundred and fifty
tons burthen, was then upon the stocks!
. . . Here were storehouses, dwelling-
houses, and various offices for the
mechanics; and every department
seemed as well filled as it could have
been in a civilised country.' (Earle,
Narrative [1966], p.66).
    Deptford Yard in England was where
Cook took charge of H.M.S. *Endeavour.*

108 Entrance of the Bay of Islands New Zealand (1827) (NK 12/66)

Inscription	'66. Entrance of the Bay of Islands New Zealand' on mount
Reverse	'Entrance of the Bay of Islands. N. Zealand'
Watercolour	23.5 x 37.5 cm
Exhibited	The Rex Nan Kivell Exhibition of Early New Zealand Pictures. Alexander Turnbull Library, Wellington, 1953 Early Watercolours of New Zealand. Auckland City Art Gallery, 1963 Rex Nan Kivell Collection Exhibition. NLA, 1974 Copy by Charles Hamilton Smith in Auckland Museum Library

Notes

The Bay of Islands is a large harbour incorporating Rangihoua, Te Puna, Kororareka, Waitangi and Paroa Bay, on the northeast coast of North Island, New Zealand.

The view appears to have been painted from two sketches, for the foreground view is of Tapeka Point, painted from Maiki Hill above the modern town of Russell. In the background is a view of nearby Mataka and Cape Wiwiki.

The compositional arrangement of the hills in the foreground recalls an earlier painting by George Tobin in the Nan Kivell Collection, entitled *Otahytey. Part of Matavai S.W. highland of Ooroomyah (Ooti Hoins) from Anchor Bay 1792.*

109 Distant View of the Bay of Islands
(1827) (NK 12/70)

Inscription	'70. Distant View of the Bay of Islands New Zealand' on mount
Reverse	'Distant View of the Bay of Islands N.Z.'
Watercolour	26 x 44.1 cm
Exhibited	Early Watercolours of New Zealand. Auckland City Art Gallery, 1963 Rex Nan Kivell Collection Exhibition. NLA, 1974

Notes

Soon after his arrival in New Zealand, Earle set out on 7 November 1827 with his friend Shand, 'having determined to proceed overland to the Bay of Islands' (Earle, *Narrative* [1966], p.67).

110 A Tabood Store House, Bay of Islands
(1827) (NK 12/69)

Inscription	'69. A Tabood Store-House at Range-hue [Rangihoua], Bay of Islands New Zealand' on mount
Reverse	'A tabood house at Range hue, Bay of Islands'
Watercolour	20.3 x 34.3 cm
Exhibited	The Rex Nan Kivell Exhibition of Early New Zealand Pictures. Alexander Turnbull Library, Wellington, 1953

Notes

'Their storehouses [or *pataka*] are generally placed upon poles, a few feet from the ground, and tabooed or consecrated' (Earle, *Narrative* [1966], p.64). This process was carried out by a priest who muttered a kind of incantation over the tabooed area. 'Great taste and ingenuity are displayed in carving and ornamenting these depositories' (Earle, *Narrative* [1966], p.64).

The Maoris possessed no adequate method of safeguarding their belongings. Important possessions such as crops and food were therefore tabooed, or rendered sacred, in order to protect them from dogs, pigs and thieves. The penalty for disturbing tabooed areas was death. 'Their food is always eaten out of little baskets, rudely woven of green flax; and as they generally leave some for their next meal, they hang these baskets on sticks or props, till they are ready to eat again . . . none of their eatables can be left on the ground, or they would become the prey of the hogs and dogs.' (Earle, *Narrative* [1966], p.64-5).

The *pa* of Rangihoua is situated in the Bay of Islands. Earle also painted the village in no. 113 and in the background of nos 111 and 112.

112 Tepoanah [Te Puna], Bay of Islands, Missionary Establishment (1827)
(NK 12/139)

Inscription '139. Tepoanah Bay of Islands New Zealand a Church Missionary Establishment' on mount l. to r. 'Green', 'woods', 'Yellow', 'Green', 'Yellow' [?], 'Green', 'land', 'light', 'sand', 'green' [?] in ink

Watercolour 32.7 x 63.2 cm
Paper scratched beneath oars to indicate wake
Three sheets joined together

Exhibited The Rex Nan Kivell Exhibition of Early New Zealand Pictures. Alexander Turnbull Library, Wellington, 1953
Early Watercolours of New Zealand. Auckland City Art Gallery, 1963
Rex Nan Kivell Collection Exhibition. NLA, 1974

Notes
The painting is a description of Rangihoua, situated near the entrance to the Bay of Islands, and of the adjoining mission, and not Te Puna as stated in the title.

In 1815, the first mission station was established in the valley (u.r.) at the foot

111 Range-hue [Rangihoua], Bay of Islands (1827) (NK 12/74)

Inscription '74. Ranghe hue, Bay of Islands, N. Zealand' on mount

Reverse 'Rangle hue, Bay of Islands/N. Zealand'

Watercolour 11.4 x 18.4 cm

Exhibited Early Watercolours of New Zealand. Auckland City Art Gallery, 1963
Copy by Charles Hamilton Smith in Auckland Museum Library

Notes
Rangihoua is about 15 km north of Kororareka. The village is depicted also in nos 110, 112 and 113.

of the mountain and village of Rangihoua (u.l.). Thomas Hanson had succeeded Peter Dillon as master of the mission ship *Active* at the time of Earle's visit.

Earle considered the war canoes (l.l.) made by the New Zealanders to be quite beautiful. 'The solidity of their structure and the carved work on them are surprising. None but men of rank are allowed to work upon them. . . . Some of their vessels were eighty feet long, and were entirely covered with beautiful carving. Their form was light and delicate. . . .' (Earle, *Narrative* [1966], p.111). The *pa* of Rangihoua is also recorded in nos 110, 111 and 113.

113 Ranghe Hue a Fortified Village New Zealand (1827) (NK 12/141)

Inscription '141. Ranghe Hue a New Zealand Fortified Village, The Residence of Warri Pork' on mount. '. . . [?] Rangehua Bay of Island New Zealand' (l.l.) . . . [?] (l.r.)
l. to r. 'clay' (u.l.), [?] (u.l.), 'light' [?] (u.c.)

Watercolour 24.1 x 59.1 cm
Two sheets joined at centre right

Exhibited The Rex Nan Kivell Exhibition of Early New Zealand Pictures. Alexander Turnbull Library, Wellington, 1953 Early Watercolours of New Zealand. Auckland City Art Gallery, 1963 Rex Nan Kivell Collection Exhibition. NLA, 1974

Notes
   The village of Rangihoua is pictured (left) overlooking the Bay of Islands. Behind the village (not in view) is the Rangihoua mission described in no. 112.

114 A New Zealand Family (1827) (NK 12/85)

Inscription '85. A New Zealand Family 1827' on mount
Watercolour 8.9 x 11.1 cm
Exhibited The Rex Nan Kivell Exhibition of Early New Zealand Pictures. Alexander Turnbull Library, Wellington, 1953 Early Watercolours of New Zealand. Auckland City Art Gallery, 1963

Notes
   Earle was most impressed by the close affection between members of families. He noted 'the general attachment of the natives of New Zealand to their wives and children. In this respect, they are far superior to most, if not all, other savages' (*Sketches Illustrative of the Native Inhabitants*, description, plate 7).

115 Residence of Shulitea, Chief of Korroradika [Kororareka] (1827-8) (NK 12/71)

Inscription	'71. The Residence of Shulitea Chief of Kororadika, Bay of Islands, New Zealand' on mount
Reverse	'The residence of Shulitea. Chief of Kororadika/Bay of Islands'
Watercolour	21.9 x 36.2 cm
Exhibited	The Rex Nan Kivell Exhibition of Early New Zealand Pictures. Alexander Turnbull Library, Wellington, 1953 Early Watercolours of New Zealand. Auckland City Art Gallery, 1963 Rex Nan Kivell Collection Exhibition. NLA, 1974

Notes

According to Earle, Kororareka Beach was the 'principal residence' of Europeans in the Bay of Islands (*Sketches Illustrative of the Native Inhabitants*, description, plate 6). Shulitea (or King George, as he preferred to call himself) was one of the first chiefs to offer protection to white men. He took care of Earle and Shand while they were living at Kororareka, and built accommodation for them. Earle described the materials and methods used in this procedure. 'They first formed the skeleton of a cottage . . . with slight sticks, firmly tied together with strips of flax . . . another party was collecting rushes . . . . These they spread in the sun for twenty-four hours . . . . They then thatched every part of the house' (Earle, *Narrative* [1966], p.105-6).

King George is probably the figure in the centre wearing the white feather head-dress.

116 Scene in Parva Bay, Bay of Islands (1827-8) (NK 12/72)

Inscription	'72. Scene in Parva Bay, Bay of Islands, N. Zealand' on mount
Reverse	'Scene in Parva bay. Bay of Islands, N. Zealand'
Watercolour	21 x 32.7 cm
Exhibited	The Rex Nan Kivell Exhibition of Early New Zealand Pictures. Alexander Turnbull Library, Wellington, 1953 Early Watercolours of New Zealand. Auckland City Art Gallery, 1963 Copy by Charles Hamilton Smith in Auckland Museum Library

Notes

The large tree has been identified by McCormick (Earle, *Narrative* [1966], p.249) as a *pohutukawa* or Christmas Tree, the best known of the New Zealand coastal trees.

117 Parva Bay, Bay of Islands (1827-8)
(NK 12/73)

Inscription	'73. Parva Bay, Bay of Islands, New Zealand' on mount
	'Land' (l.c.)
Reverse	'Parva Bay, Bay of Islands N. Zealand'
Watercolour	21 x 32.4 cm
Exhibited	Early Watercolours of New Zealand. Auckland City Art Gallery, 1963 Copy by Charles Hamilton Smith in Auckland Museum Library.

118 Bay of Islands, New Zealand
(1827-8) (NK 12/75)

Inscription	'75. Bay of Islands, New Zealand' on mount
	l. to r. 'Bay of Islands New Zealand . . . [?]' (l.r.)
Reverse	'Bay of islands, N.Z.'
Watercolour	11.4 x 37.1 cm
	Two sheets joined at centre
Exhibited	Early Watercolours of New Zealand. Auckland City Art Gallery, 1963

Notes

'The Bay of Islands is surrounded by lofty and picturesque hills, and is secured from all winds. It is full of lovely coves, and a safe anchorage is to be found nearly all over it; added to this, a number of navigable rivers are for ever emptying themselves into the Bay. . . .'
(Earle, *Narrative* [1966], p.75).

119 Wye Matte [Waimate] Waterfall, nr. the Kiddy-Kiddy [Keri-Keri] (1827-8)
(NK 12/77)

Inscription	'77. The Wye Matte, a Water Fall near the Kiddy-Kiddy, N. Zealand' on mount
Reverse	'Wye Matte, a waterfall near the Kiddy-Kiddy'
Watercolour	37.8 x 25.7 cm Scratches on surface to indicate accents in falls
Exhibited	The Rex Nan Kivell Exhibition of Early New Zealand Pictures. Alexander Turnbull Library, Wellington, 1953 Early Watercolours of New Zealand. Auckland City Art Gallery, 1963 Copy by Charles Hamilton Smith in Auckland Museum Library

Notes

The Keri-Keri waterfall and river is about 15 km west of Kororareka in the Bay of Islands. This view is further upstream from the view of Keri-Keri river in no. 130. The waterfall was generally known as the Waianiwaniwa, 'waters of the rainbow' (Earle, *Narrative* [1966], p.250).

120 The Residence of a New Zealand Chief (1827-8) (NK 12/78)

Inscription	'78. The Residence of a N. Zealand Chief' on mount
Reverse	'The residence of a N. Zealand [Chief]'
Watercolour	11.4 x 18.4 cm
Exhibited	Early Watercolours of New Zealand. Auckland City Art Gallery, 1963 Rex Nan Kivell Collection Exhibition. NLA, 1974

Notes
Generally the chief's residence was more lavishly decorated than the other huts, and embellished with carvings.

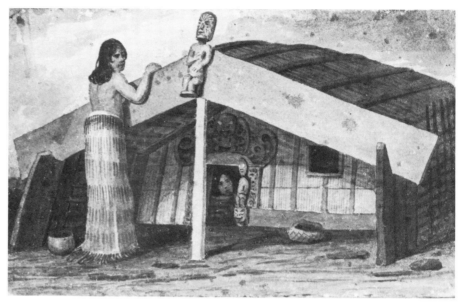

121 New Zealand Warriors and their Queen Trurero (1827-8) (NK 12/79)

Inscription	'79. New Zealand Warriors presenting Trophies of Conquest to their Queen Turero, Bay of Islands' on mount
Watercolour	11.1 x 18.4 cm
Exhibited	Early Watercolours of New Zealand. Auckland City Art Gallery, 1963 Rex Nan Kivell Collection Exhibition. NLA, 1974

Notes
These 'trophies' were the skulls of distinguished enemy chiefs killed in battle. In his narrative, Earle described the triumphant return of Atoi (a relation of King George), from a 'warlike expedition'. The trophies were presented to Queen Turero [Te Ruru], mother of King George, who is pictured sitting at the door of her house. 'They had also brought with them several heads, which they have the art of preparing, in their native ovens, so as not to disfigure the countenance nor injure the figure tattoo'd upon them . . . . These heads were decorated profusely with yellow and red ribbons, and with white feathers: they were then stuck upon short poles . . . .' (Earle, *Narrative* [1966], p.155).

122 A Tabood House belonging to Shulitea (1827-8) (NK 12/80)

Inscription	'80. A Tabood House belonging to Shulitea, Kororadica, Bay of Islands, N. Zealand' on mount
Reverse	'A Tabood House belonging to Shulitea. Kororaradica Bay of Islands N. Zealand'
Watercolour	14 x 26 cm Scratches on surface to indicate highlights
Exhibited	Early Watercolours of New Zealand. Auckland City Art Gallery, 1963

Notes
See Notes, nos 110 and 120.

123 A Tabood Store House, New Zealand (1827-8) (NK 12/81)

Inscription	'81. A Tabood Store House, New Zealand' on mount
Reverse	'A Tabood Storehouse N. Zealand'
Watercolour	25.1 x 23.5 cm

Notes
Engraved by J. Stewart for the first edition of Earle's *Narrative* (1832) (facing p.20) as *A Tabood Store House in New Zealand*.

124 A New Zealand Dancer No. 1
(1827-8) (NK 12/82)
No inscription *See* no. 125
Reverse   'Study of a N. Zealand
                     dancer'
Watercolour   15 x 11.1 cm
Exhibited   The Rex Nan Kivell
                     Exhibition of Early New
                     Zealand Pictures.
                     Alexander Turnbull
                     Library, Wellington, 1953
Notes
    Most ceremonies were concluded with
a dance or *haka*, both men and women
taking part. The dancers dressed their
hair, often pulling it up into a tight knot
on the top of their heads, with combs
of wood and bone used as decoration.
They oiled their bodies, painting or
tattooing them with red ochre and blue
paint. 'The dances of all savage nations
are beautiful, but those of the New
Zealanders partake also of the horrible
. . . the song, which always accompanies
a dance, is most harmonious. They soon
work themselves up to a pitch of
phrensy; the distortions of their face
and body are truly dreadful . . . . Love
and war are the subjects of their songs
and dances; but the details of the latter
passion are by far the most popular
among them.' (Earle, *Narrative* [1966],
p.91).

125 A New Zealand Dancer No. 2
(1827-8) (NK 12/83)
Inscription   '82. & 83. Study of New
                     Zealand Dancers' on
                     mount
                     Horizontal strip of paper
                     inscribed with title added
                     to lower edge
Reverse   'N. Zealand Dancer'
Watercolour   14.6 x 11.1 cm
Exhibited   The Rex Nan Kivell
                     Exhibition of Early New
                     Zealand Pictures.
                     Alexander Turnbull
                     Library, Wellington, 1953.

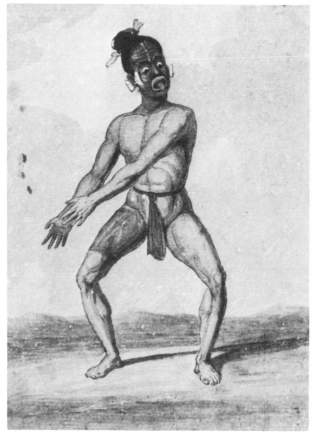

126 A New Zealand Chief (1827-8)
(NK 12/86)

Inscription   '86. A New Zeand [sic]
               Chief' on mount
Reverse   'N. Zealand Chief'
Watercolour   20 x 17.1 cm
Exhibited   Early Watercolours of
               New Zealand. Auckland
               City Art Gallery, 1963

Notes
   The chief is wearing a piece of *tapa*
cloth as ear ornamentation. The cloth is
manufactured from rare mulberry leaves.
The insufficient supply of cloth meant
that it was worn, generally only by
chiefs, as decoration rather than
clothing.

**127 A New Zealand Chief from Terra
Naky** [Taranaki] (1827-8) (NK 12/87)

Inscription   '87. A New Zealand Chief
               from Terra Naky'
               (Taranaki in another hand)
               on mount
Reverse   'A N. Zealand Chief from
               Terra Naky'
Watercolour   21.6 x 17.1 cm
Exhibited   Early Watercolours of
               New Zealand. Auckland
               City Art Gallery, 1963

Notes
   The province of Taranaki (the Maori
name for Mount Egmont) is on the west
coast of North Island.

128 Amoko a New Zealand Girl (1827-8)
(NK 12/88)

Inscription	'88. Amoko, a New Zealand Girl' on mount
Reverse	'Amoko/a New Zealand girl'
Watercolour	19 x 18.1 cm
Exhibited	Early Watercolours of New Zealand. Auckland City Art Gallery, 1963

Notes

Amoko was the daughter of a chief and, according to Earle, a good specimen of a female New Zealander. She was 'very clever; a mimic, a wit, and extremely industrious, and careful' (*Sketches Illustrative of the Native Inhabitants*, description, plate 10).

The watercolour may be the original for the engraving of Amoko in *Sketches Illustrative of the Native Inhabitants* although the latter is a more idealised version.

129 A New Zealander (1827-8)
(NK 12/89)

Inscription	'89. A New Zealander' on mount
Reverse	'New Zealander'
Watercolour	21 x 18.5 cm
Exhibited	Early Watercolours of New Zealand. Auckland City Art Gallery, 1963

Notes

Reproduced as the frontispiece to the 1832 edition of the *Narrative* and titled 'Aranghie. The Tattooer of New Zealand'.

'As this "professor" was a near neighbour of mine, I frequently paid him a visit in his "studio", and he returned the compliment whenever he had time to spare. He was considered by his country-men a perfect master in the art of tattooing, and men of the highest rank and importance were in the habit of travelling long journeys in order to put their skins under his skilful hands. Indeed, so highly were his works esteemed, that I have seen many of his drawings exhibited even after death. A neighbour of mine very lately killed a chief who had been tattoo'd by Aranghie, and, appreciating the artist's work so highly, he skinned the chieftain's thighs and covered his cartouch box with it. . . . So unrivalled is he in his profession, that a highly-finished face of a chief from the hands of this artist, is as greatly prized in New Zealand as a head from the hands of Sir Thomas Lawrence is amongst us.' (Earle, *Narrative* [1966], p.124).

130 Kiddy-Kiddy [Keri-Keri], New Zealand (1827-8) (NK 12/140)
Inscription '140. Kiddy-Kiddy. New Zealand, a Church Missionary Establishment' on mount
'. . . Kiddy-Kiddy Missionary settlement. Zealand No 2' (l.r.)
l. to r. 'clay', 'clay', 'dark heath' [?], 'clay', 'green', 'yellow', 'light Green', 'Green', 'earth', 'land', 'light', 'Green', 'Green'
Watercolour 21 x 64.1 cm
Two sheets joined at centre

Exhibited The Rex Nan Kivell Exhibition of Early New Zealand Pictures. Alexander Turnbull Library, Wellington, 1953
Early Watercolours of New Zealand. Auckland City Art Gallery, 1963
Rex Nan Kivell Collection Exhibition. NLA, 1974

Notes
Keri-Keri was situated approximately 14 kilometres south of the Rangihoua mission (no. 112). Founded in 1819, it was the second mission station in the Bay of Islands. At the time of Earle's visit in November 1827, the mission was staffed by James Kemp, George Clarke and James Hamlin. Earle was delighted to reach this 'complete little English village' (Earle, *Narrative* [1966], p.73), after travelling overland from Hokianga through thick forests and 'wild' country.

The house pictured (u.r.) is still standing. In Earle's day it was occupied by George Clarke, the other house (u.c.) belonging to James Kemp. On the extreme right of the painting, on a hill, is a Maori sepulchre. In the distance (left) are faint traces of a Maori village.

131 Crying Party, New Zealand (1827-8) (NK 12/146)
Inscription 'Crying party. N. Zealand' (l.r.) in ink; '146' on mount
Pen and ink 11.1 x 18.1 cm
Exhibited Early Watercolours of New Zealand. Auckland City Art Gallery, 1963

Notes
'All their meetings of ceremony or friendship begin with the shedding of copious floods of tears . . . .' (Earle, *Narrative* [1966], p.90). As three of the party are cutting at their bodies, it may be assumed that they are taking part in a funeral ceremony, when '. . . all gave themselves up to grief; no work was done, and not an individual was to be seen but in an agony of tears.' (Earle, *Narrative* [1966], p.167). *See also* Notes, no. 140.

132 New Zealander in his common dress
(1827-8) (NK 12/147)

Inscription	'N. Zealander in his common dress' (l.c.) in ink; '147' on mount
Pen and ink	15.9 x 10.8 cm
Exhibited	Early Watercolours of New Zealand. Auckland City Art Gallery, 1963

Notes

This is an excellent example of the basic *kahu* or foundation cloak, which was composed of long strands of the flax fibre. *See also* Notes, no. 137.

133 New Zealanders, 3 figures (1827-8)
(NK 12/148)

No inscription '148' on mount
Pen and ink   10.8 x 17.8 cm
Notes

Major Richard Cruise in his *Journal of A Ten Month's Residence in New Zealand* [1820] (Christchurch: Pegasus Press, 1957, p.35) recorded that the Maoris 'take their rest in a sitting posture, with their legs gathered under them; and from the coarse texture of the outer mat, in which they envelop themselves, they have the appearance, during the night, of a number of bee-hives scattered in groups about a village'. They no doubt also adopted these hunched-up postures as protection against the cold.

134 New Zealander (1827-8)
(NK 12/150)
No inscription '150' on mount
Pen and ink   11.4 x 10.5 cm
Notes
See Notes, no. 133.

135 New Zealanders, 2 figures (1827-8)
(NK 12/151)
No inscription '151' on mount
Pen and ink   11.1 x 15.6 cm
Exhibited   Early Watercolours of
                 New Zealand. Auckland
                 City Art Gallery, 1963.

136 Two New Zealanders Squatting

(1827-8) (NK 12/165)

Inscription   'N. Zeand [sic]' (l.l.) in
                   ink; '165' added in
                   another hand
Pen and ink   11.1 x 14.6 cm
Exhibited   Early Watercolours of
                   New Zealand. Auckland
                   City Art Gallery, 1963

Notes

The Maori (right) may have served as
a model for the squatting figure in
no. 110.

'The first thing which struck me
forcibly was, that each of these savages
was armed with a good musket . . . .'
(Earle, *Narrative* [1966], p.58). The
native (left) is shown cleaning his gun.
'Warlike stores were their grand
desideratum; and though they would
accept of any thing you chose to give
them, yet they always had hopes they
should finally receive their favourite
presents of a stocking of powder, a
piece of lead, or a musket.' (Earle,
Narrative [1966], p.200).

137 King George, New Zealand Costume (1828) (NK 12/84)

Inscription   'King George N. Zealand
                   Costume 1828' on mount
                   'N. Zealanders from
                   Nature . . . [?] Bay of
                   Islands' (l.r.)
Watercolour   10.8 x 18.4 cm
Exhibited   The Rex Nan Kivell
                   Exhibition of Early New
                   Zealand Pictures.
                   Alexander Turnbull
                   Library, Wellington, 1953
                   Early Watercolours of
                   New Zealand. Auckland
                   City Art Gallery, 1963

Notes

The watercolour shows the various
types of clothing. The natives wore only
a cloak over their naked bodies, either
thrown loosely around their shoulders
or around their waists, kilt-fashion.
There was little difference between
the clothing worn by men and women.

The cloaks were generally made of
flax, the principal crop of New Zealand.
The prepared fibre was suspended from
a plaited border in long twines, as in the
figure second from left. Cabbage-leaf
fibre was also used. Flax could be woven
to make cloaks or blankets. Dogskins
and feathers were occasionally employed

for decoration and cloak manufacture.

After 1800 an increasingly
enthusiastic reception of European goods
led to the bartering of New Zealand
produce in exchange for woollen cloaks,
which were highly prized.

The figure on the extreme left is
probably King George, wearing four
albatross feathers in his hair, a form of
embellishment favoured by chiefs. His
warriors are also wearing popular forms
of ornamentation which include feathers,
human teeth, fish teeth and pieces of
tapa cloth, as well as neck ornaments of
stones, whale bones and human bones.

138 Native of the Island of Tucopeia
(1828) (NK 12/90)
Inscription   '93. A Native of the Island
                 of Tucopea' on mount

Watercolour   24.8 x 22.2 cm
Notes
     Tucopia is one of a group of three
islands in the Pacific, near the New

Hebrides, about 170°E and 12°S. The
other two are Anuda (Cherry) and
Fataka (Mitre). Tucopia lies at 168°50'E
and 12°10'S.

139 The E.O. Racky, [Horeke] Dock Yard on the E.O. Ke Angha river (1828) (NK 12/138)

Inscription '138. The E.O. Rackey Dock Yard, on the E.O. Keangha River New Zealand' on mount 'The E.O. Racky, or Deptford Dockyard, on the E.O. Keangha River. N. Zealand, sketched in 1828' (l.c.) 'A. Earle' (l.r.)

l. to r. 'green', 'light', 'green', 'green', 'light', 'green', 'Wood', 'Dark', 'blue', 'light', 'green', 'green', 'blue' in ink

Watercolour 25.1 x 47.5 cm Two sheets joined at centre

Exhibited The Rex Nan Kivell Exhibition of Early New Zealand Pictures. Alexander Turnbull Library. Wellington, 1953 Early Watercolours of New Zealand. Auckland City Art Gallery, 1963 Rex Nan Kivell Collection Exhibition. NLA, 1974

Notes

This view was painted just before Earle left New Zealand in April 1828, probably from the deck of the *Governor Macquarie*.

140 Crying over the Bones of a Dead Chief. N. Zealand (1828) (NK 12/76)

Inscription '76. Crying over the Bones of a Dead Chief, N. Zealand' on mount 'Crying over the bones of a Dead Chief New Zealand' (l.r.) in ink

Reverse 'Crying over the bones of a dead chief'

Watercolour 17.1 x 29.5 cm

Exhibited Early Watercolours of New Zealand. Auckland City Art Gallery, 1963 Rex Nan Kivell Collection Exhibition. NLA, 1974

Notes

Such burial lamentations were known as *tangi* ceremonies. 'In the centre of this hut the bones of the deceased chief were exposed to view' (Earle, *Narrative* [1966], p.182). The bones had been left exposed for several months after which they were cleaned and decorated with feathers. 'The women here invariably perform the parts of chief mourners: a group of them, with the widow of the deceased at their head, kept up a most mournful cadence, and at every pause in their dismal song slashed their skins with a piece of shell, till their faces, necks, and arms were literally streaming down with blood. This mourning and cutting is completely a matter of business . . . .' (Earle, *Narrative* [1966], p.182).

Earle witnessed this ceremony on 2 April 1828.

141 Ballo [sic] Pyramid, Hows Island, nr. New Zealand (1828) (NK 12/65)

Inscription	'65. Ballo Pyramid, How's Island being W. by S. distance 30 miles from New Zealand, towards Port Jackson.' on mount
Reverse	'Ball's Pyramid/How's Island bearing W. by S. distance 30 miles/from N Zealand towards Port Jackson'
Watercolour	14.1 x 36.7 cm Scratches along surface to indicate highlights

Exhibited   The Rex Nan Kivell Exhibition of Early New Zealand Pictures. Alexander Turnbull Library, Wellington, 1953 Early watercolours of New Zealand. Auckland City Art Gallery, 1963

Notes

During the return voyage from New Zealand to Port Jackson in April 1828, Earle's vessel, the *Governor Macquarie*, was forced to alter course owing to strong southerly gales. 'We made Lord Howe's Islands . . . . A few miles to the southward of these islands is Ball's Pyramid, a most singular and sublime-looking rock, rising perpendicularly out of the sea to the height of a thousand feet; the base of it is enveloped in perpetual surf . . . .' (Earle, *Narrative* [1966], p.196).

142 Government House & part of the Town of Sidney [sic] (1828) (NK 12/31)

Inscription   '31. Government House and Part of the town of Sidney N.S. Wales 1828' on mount

Watercolour   18.1 x 31.1 cm

Notes

This is the original for the lithograph 'Government House and Part of the Town of Sydney' (Part II, plate 2 of Earle's *Views in New South Wales and Van Diemen's Land*, London, 1830).

In the prospectus accompanying the lithograph Earle described his subject. He stressed the beauty of 'its situation, the gardens, and domain around it', rather than the building itself, which he considered 'mean' in appearance. He paid tribute to Mrs Macquarie's taste in designing the garden according to picturesque conventions. The wallabies are not examples of 'artistic licence' but were part of Mrs Macquarie's original intention. Earle has also included examples of Australian flora (the Australian speargrass and the Norfolk Pine), which would appear exotic to English eyes.

143 Umatak Harbour, Island of Guam, one of the Ladrones (1828) (NK 12/116)

Inscription   '116. Umatak Harbour, Island Guam, one of the Ladrones' on mount

Watercolour   24.7 x 52.8 cm
               Upper section joined to painting

Exhibited   Rex Nan Kivell Collection Exhibition. NLA, 1974

Notes

On 12 October 1828, Earle left Sydney aboard the *Rainbow*, bound for India. The vessel called at the Ladrones Islands, Guam, Manila, Singapore and Madras.

Umatac harbour is on the east coast of Guam. During the nineteenth century, many scientists, voyagers, whalers and foreign ships visited Guam. Between 1817 and 1828, the island was visited by three scientific expeditions, including the scientists Kotzebue, Freycinet and d'Urville.

The house pictured (u.l.) was the Spanish governor's summer villa.

144 Umatak, Island of Guam (1828) (NK 12/121)

Inscription   '121. Umatack, Island of Guam' on mount

Watercolour   21.6 x 27.3 cm
               Horizontal panel added (top) with vertical panel added (right)

Exhibited   Rex Nan Kivell Collection Exhibition. NLA, 1974

Notes

The view is taken from the side of the bay opposite that of no. 143. The Spanish governor's summer villa is visible, partly obscured, at left.

145 A Woman of the Mariannas or Ladrone Islands (1828) (NK 12/124)

Inscription   '124. A Woman of the Mariannas or Ladrone Islands, Scraping Yams to make Paste for Bread; — Drawn from nature' on mount

Watercolour   14.9 x 18 cm

Exhibited   Rex Nan Kivell Collection Exhibition. NLA, 1974

Notes
   The Marianas or Ladrones Islands are situated in the Pacific Ocean north of the Caroline Islands.

146 Malacca (1828) (NK 12/118)

Inscription   '118. Malacca.'

Watercolour   21.6 x 48.3 cm
                         Vertical panel added to left side. Horizontal panel added to top of painting

Exhibited   Rex Nan Kivell Collection Exhibition. NLA, 1974

Notes
   On the right is the Stadthuis Square and the Christchurch — a reminder of the Dutch occupation of Malacca from 1640 until 1795, when the British took over. On the extreme right men are at work remodelling the Stadthuis. There is a lithograph by Arthus Bertrand of the completed building in February 1847 (*see* John Bastin and C. A. Gibson-Hill, 'Five Early Watercolour Sketches of Penang & Malacca': *Journal of the Malayan Branch of the Royal Asiatic Society* 31 (1958): 163-71).

147 Malacca (1828) (NK 12/119)
Inscription   '119. Malacca.' on mount
Reverse   'Malacca'
Watercolour   19.7 x 34 cm
              Vertical panel added
              (right)

Exhibited   Rex Nan Kivell Collection
              Exhibition. NLA, 1974

148 Distant View of Malacca (1828)
(NK 12/120)
Inscription   '120. Distant View of
              Malacca, 1828'
Watercolour   10.6 x 34.9 cm
              Two sheets joined
              together at centre.

149 View in Pulo Penang or Prince Edward's Island (1828) (NK 12/122)
Inscription   '122. View in Pulo Penang
               or Prince Edward's Island'
               on mount
               'Grass' [?] (l.c.)

Watercolour   25.8 x 52.4 cm
               Horizontal panel added
               (top)

Exhibited   Rex Nan Kivell Collection
               Exhibition. NLA, 1974

Notes
    Part of Fort Cornwallis is visible
(right) with two sentries on the
ramparts.

150 Water Fall, Penang (1828)
(NK 12/117)
Inscription   '117. Water Fall. Penang'
               on mount
               L. to r. 'black' [?] (u.c.),
               [. . .?] (u.c.), 'lush' [?]
               (u.r.)
Reverse   'Waterfall at Penang'
Watercolour   37.5 x 27 cm
Notes
    'The waterfall at Penang is also
featured in the very accurate series of
tinted lithographs prepared by Wm
Daniell from water-colour drawings
executed by Capt. Robert Smith. . . .
There is no waterfall of this form on the
island now . . .' (Bastin and Gibson-Hill,
J.M.B.R.A.S., p.167).

151 A catamaran Madras Roads (1829)
(NK 12/126)
Inscription '126. A Catamaran,
Madras Roads' on mount

Watercolour 14.6 x 26.3 cm
Scratches in paint (fore-
ground) to indicate
highlights
Exhibited Rex Nan Kivell Collection
Exhibition. NLA, 1974

Notes
To the right is a British sailing ship at
anchor. The Indian at the right appears
to be negotiating the sale of three
chickens to someone on the ship from
which the scene was painted.

**152 Bullock Hackery, Madras, the
original outline** (1829) (NK 12/156)
Inscription '156' on mount
'1829 Madras' (l.l.) 'blue'
(u.r.) in ink
Pen and ink 15.9 x 21.3 cm.

**153 A Bullock Hackery or Cow Coach
of India** (1829) (NK 12/125)

Inscription	'125. A Bullock Hackery or Cow Coach of India' on mount. 'Mad . . .' l.r. corner, in ink
Watercolour	18.7 x 17.1 cm
Exhibited	Rex Nan Kivell Collection Exhibition. NLA, 1974.

**154 Bullock Hackery, or Cow Coach of
India** (1829) (NK 12/127)

Inscription	'127. A Bullock Hackery or Cow Coach of India' on mount. 'White' (u.c.) 'blue' (u.c.)
Watercolour	21 x 26.8 cm
Exhibited	Rex Nan Kivell Collection Exhibition. NLA, 1974

155 Napoleons Tomb in the Island of St. Helena (1829) (NK 12/142)

Inscription   '142. Napoleon's Tomb in the Island of St. Helena' on mount

Watercolour   26.7 x 42.9 cm

Reverse   Two small pencil sketches of women's heads (profile view)

Exhibited   Rex Nan Kivell Collection Exhibition. NLA, 1974

Notes

     H. E. Spencer (*Augustus Earle*, p. 485) has pointed out that the only time Earle was in the vicinity of St Helena was during his voyage from Mauritius to England, late in 1829.

156 Cape Tennets (Date unknown) (NK 12/145)

No inscription '145' on mount

Watercolour   20 x 34 cm

Notes

     According to Spencer (*Augustus Earle*, p.486), this may be the port of Santa Cruz, Teneriffe, in the Canary Islands. Earle stopped there with the *Beagle* on 6 January 1832. The sea-wall resembles that of Santa Cruz. as does the general appearance of the town.

157 Dunluce Castle County of Antrim, Ireland (Date unknown) (NK 12/143)

Inscription	'143. Dunluce Castle County of Antrim Ireland'
Reverse	'Dunluce Castle/County Antrim/near the Giants Causeway'
Watercolour	28.6 x 37.8 cm
Exhibited	Rex Nan Kivell Collection Exhibition. NLA, 1974

Notes

The steam vessel (t.l.) is of a late 1830s design. Earle visited Ireland before he died in 1838.

158 (Cape Tennets) Castle Dawson, Derry, Ireland (Date unknown) (NK 12/144)

Inscription	'144. Castle Dawson, Derry, Ireland' on mount
Watercolour	18.7 x 32.4 cm
Exhibited	Rex Nan Kivell Collection Exhibition. NLA, 1974

This work no doubt was also painted during Earle's trip to Ireland before he died in 1838.

159 Scene from Roderick Random

(Date unknown) (NK 12/133)

Inscription	'133. Scene from Roderick Random' on mount 'Roderick Random discovering his Uncle Lieut. Bowling in poverty and distress in France' (l.r.) in ink
Pen and ink and wash	17.8 x 26.7 cm

Notes

Tobias Smollett's *Roderick Random* was published in 1748. Rowlandson also painted a version of this scene (*see* George M. Kahrl, *Tobias Smollett Traveler-Novelist* (New York: Octagon, 1968), quoted by H. E. Spencer (*Augustus Earle*, p.493). The monotone nature of the drawing suggests that with no. 160 it may have been a preliminary study for an engraving and intended for publication.

160 Scene from Peregrine Pickle

(Date unknown) (NK 12/134)

Inscription	'134. Scene from Peregrine Pickle' on mount 'Lieut Hatchway' (l.l.), 'Commodore Trunnion' (l.c.), 'Mr Gamaliel Pickle/ Vide Peregrine Pickle' (l.r.) in ink
Pen and ink and wash	17.8 x 26.7 cm

Notes

This novel by Tobias Smollett was published in 1751. Thomas Stothard painted a version of this scene in the frontispiece to the first edition.

Behind the three men in the foreground sits Tom Pipes, gazing at an ostrich egg.

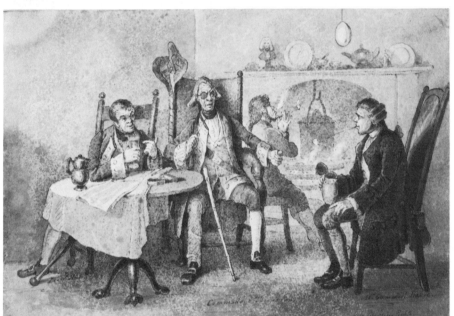

161 First sight of the Pacific Coast from America (Date unknown) (NK 12/135)
No inscription '135.' on mount
Pen and ink   17.8 x 26.7 cm
and wash
Notes

In the foreground, standing on a rock with his arms outstretched, is a man, probably Balboa, in the uniform of a conquistador. In the background are Indians and more conquistadores.

In 1513 Balboa found a passage to the Pacific Ocean. 'That extraordinary but unfortunate man was the first European whose eyes rested on the broad Pacific. He had heard from the Indians of its existence, and resolutely set out to discover it, well aware of the dangers and difficulties he had to encounter' (Graham, *Journal of a Voyage to Brazil* 1969, p.5). *See also* John Keats, 'On first looking into

Chapman's Homer' (October 1816):
  Or like stout Cortez when with eagle eyes
  He stared at the Pacific — and all his men
  Looked at each other with a wild surmise —
  Silent, upon a peak in Darien.

The poem (Keats has substituted Cortez's name for Balboa's) reflects the general interest in exploration and discovery during the nineteenth century, evident in both literature and painting.

162 Robinson Crusoe (Date unknown) (NK 12/157)
No inscription '157' on mount
Pen and ink   11.4 x 14 cm
and wash
Notes

Earle may have intended to publish an engraved version of this sketch, possibly to illustrate an edition of *Robinson Crusoe*.

163 Two female heads, Portraits (Date unknown) (NK 12/158)
No inscription '158'
Watercolour   10.8 x 22.9 cm
Notes

Shoulders and sleeves of the woman (right) are lightly sketched in pencil.

An analysis of the hairstyles of both the women, and of the jewellery and costume of the European lady on the left, would indicate a late 1820s date. Earle no doubt sketched the two women when he visited India and the Pacific during 1828-30.

164 Portrait of a Lady (Date unknown)
(NK 12/159)
No inscription '159' on mount
Watercolour   26 x 23.8 cm
                    Lower right section (table)
                    together with a portion of
                    the hands and the bracelet
                    on the left arm are
                    sketched in pencil
                    Other unfinished areas
                    include the edges of the
                    belt, and dress neckline
                    (l.l.) corner torn away
Notes
    The jewellery, dress and hairstyle are
of the period 1828-30. This portrait may
have been painted in Madras, where
Earle spent some time during this period.

165 Portrait of a Gentleman
(Date unknown) (NK 12/160)
No inscription '160' on mount
Watercolour   17.8 x 17.1 cm
                    Collar and cravat sketched
                    in pencil.

166 The Head of a Gentleman, a Portrait
(Date unknown) (NK 12/163)
No inscription '163'
Watercolour   14 x 13.3 cm
                                Jacket sketched in pencil
Notes
　　The identity of the gentleman remains obscure. Although the portrait was originally believed to be of Captain Piper, it does not resemble Earle's oil portrait of that gentleman. The man in this portrait appears to be younger than Captain Piper.

167 Untitled watercolour
(Date unknown) (NK 11025)
No inscription Signed 'A. Earle' (l.r.) on
                                mount
Watercolour   9.1 x 14.7 cm
Notes
　　The scenery depicted seems to be in the Swiss or Italian Alps, or the Lake District; the latter is more probable, as Earle made a trip to the district in 1813. Stylistically, this painting seems to be an early work and may date from the 1813 period.
　　Rex Nan Kivell bought the watercolour independently of the main body of watercolours in the collection. In a letter dated 20 May 1975, he records that it belonged to a scrap-book of miscellaneous prints and drawings which he purchased at a Sotheby's sale in 1955.

168 Attributed to Augustus Earle
View Near Rio Janeiro (Date unknown)
(Petherick Collection)
Inscription   Unsigned and undated
Watercolour   16.1 x 24.2 cm
Notes

    The painting was purchased by E. A. Petherick at an auction held by James Rimell and Son, London, in 1887. In the catalogue the painter is listed as Edward Dayes. This seems unlikely, as Dayes never visited South America. Moreover, the watercolour closely resembles Earle's work. The vaguely defined background forms (the mountain scenery) and the foreground figures remind one of Earle's watercolours of Rio. The drawing of the palm trees, foreground foliage, and the road (l.l.) curving into depth are stylistically similar to the Blue Mountain and Illawarra watercolours.

Appendix 1: Chronology

1789	James Earl, an American portrait-painter (the younger brother of Ralph Earl), married Caroline Smyth (widow of Joseph Smyth, an American Tory) in London; James Earl admitted to the Royal Academy. (The only extant portrait by James Earl remains at the Charleston Art Gallery)	
1793	Birth of Augustus Earle	
1796	James Earl returned to America. He died of yellow fever at Charleston	
1806	For the next few years, Augustus Earle exhibited at the Royal Academy. His name appears regularly on the Academy lists and he took lessons there. Fellow-students included Americans C. R. Leslie and S. F. B. Morse	*Judgement of Midas* (after Ovid, location unknown)
1808		*Battle of Poitiers* (location unknown)
1809		*Caius Marcius taking Possession of the City of Corioli* (location unknown)
1811		*Banditti* (location unknown)
1812		*Banditti* (location unknown)
1813	Earle and Morse embarked on a sketching trip around Deal	
1814		*A Man-of-War's Boats Cutting out a French Barque* (location unknown)
1815–16	End of the Napoleonic Wars. This led to increased travelling in the Mediterranean. Earle obtained a passage on a storeship bound for Sicily and Malta. He visited North Africa, Sicily, Malta, Gibraltar and sketched the ruins of Carthage and Ptolemeia, Malta and Sicily	*View of the Harbour and Part of the Town of Calais* (private collection). Provided sketches for an aquatint entitled *The Grand Harbour of Valetta* (private collection). Painted a watercolour *Ruins of Leptis Magna* (Royal Collection, Windsor Castle)

1817   Returned to England

1818   Left for New York, in March.
He worked there for some
months, then moved to
Philadelphia

July: Exhibited two paintings in
the Pennsylvania Academy of Fine
Arts. These were *Full Length
Portrait of a Gentleman* and
Portrait of a Gentleman (location
unknown)

1820–4   In February 1820 sailed for Rio
de Janeiro, where he remained
until 1824. Visited Chile in
June 1820 and was in Lima
from July to December 1820.
Met the well-known English
writer, Maria Graham
Left Rio in February 1824 for
the Cape of Good Hope, bound
thence for Calcutta. Earle had
a letter of introduction to Lord
Amherst, Governor-General of
India. 26 March 1824: *Duke of
Gloucester* forced to anchor off
Tristan da Cunha. Earle
stranded there until 29
November 1824, when he left
island on board the *Admiral
Cockburn*

Painted *Divine Service on Board a
British Frigate* (H.M.S. *Hyperion*,
1820) watercolour study in the
Rex Nan Kivell Collection (no. 12).
Oil version exhibited at the Royal
Academy, now in the National
Maritime Museum, Greenwich
Exhibited at the Royal Academy
Gate of Pernambuco in Brazil,
painted in 1821 (location
unknown). Illustrated Maria
Graham's *Journal of a Voyage to
Brazil* (London 1824). Water-
colours of Brazil in the Rex Nan
Kivell Collection (nos 15-36). *See*
the watercolours of Tristan da
Cunha (nos 38-53), and Earle's *A
Narrative of A Nine Months'
Residence in New Zealand in 1827;
Together With a Journal of a
Residence in Tristan D'Acunha, an
Island Situated Between South
America and the Cape of Good
Hope* (London: Longman, 1832)
Noted the 'perfect park scenery' of
June Park, Van Dieman's Land . . .
(no. 57). Painted watercolours
including *Cape Barathus
Adventure Bay V.D. Land* (no. 56).
Also made sketches for litho-
graphic views and panorama of the
island (published and exhibited in
1831)
Painted portraits

1825   18 January: Arrived in
Tasmania. 14 May: Arrived in
Sydney on brig *Cyprus* and in
October, engaged to redecorate
the dining room for Governor
Brisbane's farewell banquet
(*Sydney Gazette*, 31 October
1825)

1826   July: Advertised the opening
of his art gallery. Exhibition
described by McGarvie in
October in his diary (ML
A1332 p. 235) and in his article
'On the State of the Fine Arts
in New South Wales' (*Sydney
Gazette*, 28 and 30 July 1829),
written under the pseudonym
'A.B. Marramatta'.
Sold tickets for a subscription
concert

August: Obtained lithographic press and began publishing a set of Australian views (*see Sydney Monitor,* 11 August 1826, *Sydney Gazette,* 28 August 1826)

Journeyed to the Blue Mountains, Bathurst, and the Wellington Valley, the Hunter River, Port Stephens and Port Macquarie

Painted watercolours of these regions. Painted illusionistic scenery (classical statues of Apollo and Minerva) around the 'theatre' above the old courthouse in Castlereagh Street. Probably sketched the watercolour scenes for Burford's panorama of Hobart (exhibited in London, 1831)

1827

February: Painted eight views from the top of Palmer's Hill, Sydney, which Burford used for his panorama of Sydney

April-May: made a sketching trip to the Illawarra district. Fell from his horse and broke his leg

October: Left for New Zealand in the *Governor Macquarie*

(*see* nos 104-37 and 139-41)

1828 5 May: Returned to Sydney in the *Governor Macquarie*

12 October: Left Sydney in the *Rainbow*. Visited the Caroline Islands, Guam, Manila, Singapore and Madras. Ill health forced him to leave Madras in *La Julie,* which was condemned at Mauritius in July 1829

Watercolours (nos 143-54). In Madras made sketches for a panorama

1830 Returned to England in the *Resource*

Executed a series of views for a panorama of Mauritius

Published *Views in New South Wales and Van Diemen's Land* (London)

1831 28 October: Appointed as Artist Supernumerary with victuals on the *Beagle* on surveying trip to southern coasts of America (perhaps due to the influence of his half-brother, Admiral W. H. Smyth). Sailed on 27 December 1831

1832 Reached Rio on 4 April 1832. Continued ill health forced Earle to resign his post. He returned to London some time after November 1833

Published *A Narrative of a Nine Months' Residence in New Zealand in 1827; Together With a Journal of a Residence in Tristan D'Acunha . . .* (London, Longman, 1832)

1837

Exhibited at the Royal Academy: *Life on the ocean, representing the usual occupation of the young officers in the steerage of a British frigate at sea,* watercolour study (based on no. 13). Oil version in the National Maritime Museum. Also painted *Divine Service as it is usually performed on board a British frigate at sea* (based on no. 12)

1838

A Bivouac of Travellers in Australia, in a Cabbage-tree Forest, day break (no. 3). Published *Sketches Illustrative of the Native Inhabitants and Islands of New Zealand* . . .(London, R. Martin and Co.), ten coloured lithographs

10 December: Died in London, of 'asthma and debility'

Burford painted a panorama of the Bay of Islands, after drawings by Earle

Appendix 2 : Some paintings in other collections

View of the Harbour and part of the town of Calais. 1815, oil. Measurements
   unavailable. Private collection.
The Ruins of Leptis Magna. 1816, watercolour. 34.9 x 54.3 cm. Windsor
   Castle.
Slave Market in Rio. 1823, watercolour. 18.4 x 26.5 cm. British Museum.
View of Hobart. c.1825-7, watercolour. Measurements unavailable. Sydney,
   Mitchell Library.
Six watercolour studies for a panorama of Hobart and vicinity, c.1825-7.
   36.8 x 54.6 cm. Sydney, Mitchell Library.
Sydney from the Heights of North Sydney. c.1825-7, oil. 40.6 x 79.7 cm.
   Sydney, Dixson Library.
View of Port Jackson taken from the Flag Staff, Sydney. c.1825-7, watercolour.
   13.9 x 36.8 cm. Sydney, Mitchell Library.
*Portrait of Arangi Tooker Chief of Cower Cower Bay of Islands,
   New Zealand, with his wife and son.* 1827, oil. 84 x 65cm.
   Wellington, Alexander Turnbull Library.
*Meeting of the artist and Hongi at the Bay of Islands,
   November 1827.* 1827, oil. 57.5 x 86.5cm. Wellington,
   Alexander Turnbull Library.
Cower Cower River. 1827, watercolour. 23.5 x 53.5cm. Wellington,
   Alexander Turnbull Library.
Midshipmans Berth. 1837, oil. 58.4 x 88.9 cm. National Maritime Museum,
   London.
Bible Reading on Board. 1837, oil. 55.9 x 87.6 cm. National Maritime Museum,
   London.

Portraits
Sir Thomas Brisbane. 1825-6, oil. 261 x 149.9 cm. Sydney, Mitchell Library.
Major Frederick Goulburn. 1825-6, oil. 83.5 x 67.3 cm. Sydney, Parliament
   House.
John Mackaness. 1825-6, oil. 45.4 x 32.7 cm (as mounted on board), 36.8 x
   27.3 cm (original fragment). Sydney, Mitchell Library.
Dr Robert Townson. 1825-6, oil. 81.3 x 64.8 cm. Sydney, Mitchell Library.
Captain John Piper. c.1826, oil. 192.4 x 120.6 cm. Sydney, Mitchell Library.
Mrs John Piper and her Children. c.1826, oil. 194.3 x 121.3 cm. Sydney,
   Mitchell Library.
Richard Brooks. 1826-7, oil. 73.7 x 61 cm. Australian National Gallery.
Mrs Richard Brooks. 1826-7, oil. 73.7 x 61 cm. Australian National Gallery.
Captain Thomas Valentine Blomfield. 1827, oil. 33 x 26.7 cm. Private collec-
   tion.
Col. William Stewart. Date unknown, oil. 28.6 x 20.9 cm. Sydney, Mitchell
   Library.

Bibliography

Manuscript sources

Earle, Augustus, Certified copy of entry of death, Somerset House, London.
Letter to Mrs Ward, 19 May 1827, Ae 23, Mitchell Library, Sydney.
MS list of titles of watercolours by A. Earle. National Library of Australia.
Notes on family portrait group (mother and three children) supposedly painted by Augustus Earle. PXN 151, Mitchell Library, Sydney.

McGarvie, J., Diary. A 1332, Mitchell Library, Sydney.

Richardson, J. L., Letter to the Rev. Samuel Marsden, 4 April 1829, Marsden Papers, A 1992, Mitchell Library, Sydney.

Townson, R., Letter to T. Reddall, n.d. Reddall Papers, A 423, Mitchell Library, Sydney.
Notes on portrait of Dr R. Townson, by Mr D. Setelik, July 1964, PXN 2, Mitchell Library, Sydney.

Printed sources

Abbey, John Roland, *Travel in Aquatint and Lithography, 1770-1860, from the Library of J. R. Abbey: A Bibliographical Catalogue.* 2 vols. London: Maggs, 1956-7.

Allott, Miriam (Farris), *The Poems of John Keats.* Harlow: Longman, 1970.

Barbier, Carl, *William Gilpin: His Drawings, Teaching and Theory of the Picturesque.* Oxford: Clarendon Press, 1963.

Bastin, John and Gibson-Hill, C. A., 'Five Early Watercolour Sketches of Penang & Malacca.' *Journal of the Malayan Branch of the Royal Asiatic Society* 31 (1958): 163-71.

Bayley, William A., *Green Meadows: Centenary History of the Shellharbour Municipality, New South Wales.* Albion Park, NSW: Shellharbour Municipal Council, 1959.

—— *Blue Haven: Centenary History of Kiama Municipality, New South Wales.* Kiama: Municipal Council, 1960.

Boase, T. S. R., *English Art, 1800-1870.* Oxford History of Art series, vol. 10. Oxford: Clarendon Press, 1959.

Booy, Derrick Miles, *Rock of Exile: A Narrative of Tristan da Cunha.* London: Dent, 1957.

Botting, Douglas, *Humboldt and the Cosmos.* London: Joseph, 1973.

Burford, Robert, *Description of a View of the Town of Sydney, New South Wales, the Harbour of Port Jackson and Surrounding Country.* Painted by R. Burford after drawings by Augustus Earle with an accompanying description. London: J. and C. Adlard, 1830.

—— *Description of a View of Hobart Town, Van Diemen's Land, and the Surrounding Country.* Painted by R. Burford after drawings by Augustus Earle with an accompanying description. London: G. Nicols, 1831.

—— *Description of a View of the Bay of Islands, New Zealand, and the Surrounding Country*. Painted by R. Burford from drawings taken by Augustus Earle. London: G. Nicols, 1838.

Burke, Edmund, *A Philosophical Enquiry into the Origin of Our Ideas of the Sublime and Beautiful*, edited by J. T. Boulton. London: Routledge and Kegan Paul, 1958.

Burke, Joseph, and Caldwell, Colin, *Hogarth: The Complete Engravings*. London: Thames and Hudson, 1968.

Bury, Adrian, *Francis Towne: Lone Star of Water-Colour Painting*. London: Skilton, 1962.

—— *Two Centuries of British Water-Colour Painting*. London: Newnes, 1950.

Buscombe, Eve, 'Artists and Their Sitters: a Colonial Portrait; a Guide to the Portrait Painters of New South Wales and Van Diemen's Land, 1820-1850.' M.A. thesis, Australian National University, 1970.

Carano, Paul, and Sanchez, Pedro C., *A Complete History of Guam*. Rutland, Vt.: Tuttle, 1964.

Clark, C. M. H., *A History of Australia*. Melbourne: Melbourne University Press, 1962.

Clark, Kenneth, *Landscape into Art*. London: Murray, 1949.

Cunningham, Peter, *Two Years in New South Wales: A Series of Letters Comprising Sketches of the Actual State of Society in That Colony, of its Peculiar Advantages to Emigrants, of its Topography, Natural History, etc.* 2 vols. London: Henry Colburn, 1827.

Cunnington, Cecil Willett, and Cunnington, Phillis, *Handbook of English Costume in the Nineteenth Century*. London: Faber, 1959.

Darwin, Charles, *Charles Darwin and the Voyage of the Beagle: Letters and Notebooks*. Edited, with an introduction by Nora Barlow. London: Pilot Press, 1945.

—— *Diary of the Voyage of H.M.S. Beagle*, edited by Nora Barlow. Cambridge: Cambridge University Press, 1933.

Davidson, Angus, *Edward Lear, Landscape Painter and Nonsense Poet (1812-1888)*. London: Murray, 1938.

De Terra, Helmut, *Humboldt: The Life and Times of Alexander von Humboldt, 1769-1859*. New York: Knopf, 1955.

Defoe, Daniel, *The Life and Strange Surprising Adventures of Robinson Crusoe . . . Being a Facsimile reprint of the first edition published in 1719*. London: Elliot Stock, 1883.

Dixson, W., 'Notes on Australian Artists, pt. 2.' *Journal and Proceedings of the Royal Australian Historical Society* 4 (1919): 283-300.

Docking, Gilbert, *Two Hundred Years of New Zealand Painting*. Wellington: Reed, 1971.

Dunlap, William, *History of the Rise and Progress of the Arts of Design in the United States*. 3 vols. 3rd ed. New York: Benjamin Blom, 1965.

Dutton, Geoffrey, *White on Black: The Australian Aborigine Portrayed in Art*. South Melbourne, Vic.: Macmillan of Australia in association with the Art Gallery Board of South Australia, 1974.

Earle, Augustus, *A Narrative of A Nine Months' Residence in New Zealand in 1827; Together With a Journal of a Residence in Tristan D'Acunha, an Island Situated Between South America and the Cape of Good Hope*. London: Longman, 1832.

—— *Narrative of a Residence in New Zealand and Journal of a Residence in Tristan da Cunha*, edited by E. H. McCormick, London: Oxford University Press, 1966.

Contemporary reviews of Narrative:
>   *Protestant Journal* nos 1-4, London, 1833.
>   *Quarterly Review* no. xcv, London, 1832.
>   *Westminster Review* no. xvii, London, 1832.

—— *Sketches Illustrative of the Native Inhabitants and Islands of New Zealand, from Original Drawings.* Published under the auspices of the New Zealand Association by R. Martin & Co., London, 1838.

—— *Views in Australia.* Sydney, 1826.

—— *Views in New South Wales, and Van Diemen's Land: Australian Scrap Book, 1830.* London: J. Cross, 1830.

Earle, Pliny, *Ralph Earle and His Descendants.* Worcester: Charles Hamilton, 1888.

Eitner, Lorenz, 'The open window and the storm-tossed boat: an essay in the iconography of Romanticism.' *Art Bulletin* 37 (1953): 281-90.

Fairchild, Hoxie Neale, *The Noble Savage: A Study in Romantic Naturalism.* New York: Russell & Russell, 1961.

Fawcett, Trevor, *The Rise of English Provincial Art: Artists, Patrons and Institutions outside London, 1800-1830.* Oxford: Clarendon Press, 1974.

Ferguson, John, *Bibliography of Australia.* V.I-IV (1784-1850). Canberra: National Library, 1975-6.

Field, Barron, *Geographical Memoirs on New South Wales, by various hands...* London: John Murray, 1825.

FitzRoy, Robert, *Narrative of the Surveying Voyages of His Majesty's Ships Adventure and Beagle, between the Years 1826 and 1836, Describing Their Examination of the Southern Shores of South America, and the Beagle's Circumnavigation of the Globe.* 3 vols. London: Henry Colburn, 1839.

Flower, Cedric, *Duck & Cabbage Tree, A Pictorial History of Clothes in Australia, 1788-1914.* Sydney: Angus and Robertson, 1968.

Gardner, A. T. E., *History of Water-Color Painting in America.* New York: Reinhold Publishing Corp., 1966.

Gaunt, William, *A Concise History of English Painting.* London: Thames and Hudson, 1970.

Gillray, James, *The Works of James Gillray from the Original Plates.* London: A. G. John, 1897.

Gilpin, William, *Three Essays: On Picturesque Beauty; On Picturesque Travel; and, On Sketching Landscape: To which is added a Poem, on Landscape Painting.* 2 vols. London: R. Blamire, 1792.

Gombrich, Ernst, *Art and Illusion: A Study in the Psychology of Pictorial Representation.* Princeton: Princeton University Press, 1969.

Gower, Ronald, *Sir David Wilkie.* London: George Bell, 1902.

Graham, Maria, *Journal of a Voyage to Brazil, and Residence There, During Part of the Years 1821, 1822, 1823.* New York: Frederick A. Praeger, 1969.

Graves, Algernon, *The British Institution, 1806-1867: A Complete Dictionary of Contributors and Their Work from the Foundation of the Institution.* Bath: Kingsmead Reprints, 1969.

—— *A Dictionary of Artists Who Have Exhibited Works in Principal London Exhibitions, 1760-1893.* Bath: Kingsmead Reprints, 1969.

—— *The Royal Academy of Arts. A Complete Dictionary of Contributors and their Work from its Foundation in 1769 to 1904.* Bath: Kingsmead Reprints, 1969.

Hardie, Martin, *Water-Colour Painting in Britain.* Edited by Dudley Snelgrove with Jonathon Mayne and Basil Taylor. 2 vols. London: Batsford, 1967.

Harley, Rosamond, *Artists' Pigments c.1600-1835: A Study in English Documentary Sources*. London: Butterworths, 1970.

Harris, Alexander, *Settlers and Convicts: or, Recollections of Sixteen Years' Labour in the Australian Backwoods*. By An Emigrant Mechanic. London: C. Cox, 1847.

Harris, Max, and Forbes, Alison, *The Land That Waited*. Melbourne: Lansdowne, 1967.

Heintzelman, Arthur W., *The Watercolour Drawings of Thomas Rowlandson, from the Albert H. Wiggin Collection in the Boston Public Library*. New York: Watson-Guptill, 1971.

Henderson, James, *A History of the Brazil: Comprising its Geography, Commerce, Colonization, Aboriginal Inhabitants &c*. London: Longman etc., 1821.

Hipple, Walter J., *The Beautiful, the Sublime and the Picturesque in Eighteenth-Century British Aesthetic Theory*. Carbondale, Ill.: Southern Illinois University Press, 1957.

Humboldt, Alexander von, *Kosmos, A General Survey of the Physical Phenomena of the Universe*. 2 vols. London: Bailliere, 1845.

Hussey, Christopher, *The Picturesque*. London: G. P. Putman & Sons, 1927.

James, David, 'An English Painter in First Empire Brazil, with Catalogue of the Brazilian Works of Augustus Earle' translated by G. Brodsky, *Revista do Patrimonio Historico e Artistico Nacional*, vol. 12. Rio de Janeiro, 1955.

Kahrl, George M., *Tobias Smollett Traveler-Novelist*. New York: Octagon Books, 1968.

Laver, James, *English Costume of the Nineteenth Century*. London: A. & C. Black, 1950.

Lear, Edward, *Edward Lear in Greece: Journals of a Landscape Painter in Greece and Albania*. London: Kimber, 1965.

—— *Edward Lear in Southern Italy: Journals of a Landscape Painter in Southern Calabria and the Kingdom of Naples*. London: Kimber, 1964.

—— *Indian Journal: Watercolours and Extracts from the Diary of Edward Lear (1873-1875)*, edited by Ray Murphy. London: Jarrolds, 1953.

Lewis, Michael, *The Navy in Transition 1814-1864: A Social History*. London: Hodder & Stoughton, 1965.

Lindsay, Jack, *Death of the Hero: French Painting from David to Delacroix*. London: Studio, 1961.

Lister, Raymond, *British Romantic Art*. London: Bell, 1973.

Mackay, Margaret, *Angry Island: The Story of Tristan da Cunha, 1506-1963*. London: Barker, 1963.

Mead, Sidney Moko, *Traditional Maori Clothing: A Study of Technological and Functional Change*. Wellington: Reed, 1969.

Moore, Doris Langley, *Fashion Through Fashion Plates, 1771-1970*. London: Ward Lock, 1971.

Moorehead, Alan, *Darwin and the Beagle*. London: Hamish Hamilton, 1969.

Morse, Edward, *Samuel F. B. Morse; His Letters and Journals*. Boston: Houghton Mifflin, 1914.

Mourot, Suzanne, *This Was Sydney — A Pictorial History from 1788 to the Present Time*. Sydney: Ure Smith, 1969.

Murray-Oliver, Anthony, *Augustus Earle in New Zealand*. Christchurch: Whitcombe & Tombs, 1968.

O'Shaughnessy, Peter; Inson, Graeme, and Ward, Russel, *The Restless Years: Being Some Impressions of the Origin of the Australian*. Brisbane: Jacaranda, 1968.

Parris, Leslie, *Landscape in Britain, c.1750-1850*. London: Tate Gallery, 1973.

Payne-Knight, Richard, *The Landscape, A Didactic Poem, in Three Books*. London: R. Bulmer, 1794.

Price, Sir Uvedale, *An Essay on the Picturesque as Compared with the Sublime and the Beautiful: And on the Use of Studying Pictures for the Purpose of Improving Real Landscape*. 2 vols. London: Hereford, 1794-8.

Quennell, Peter, *Romantic England: Writing and Painting, 1717-1851*. London: Weidenfeld and Nicolson, 1970.

Redgrave, Richard, and Redgrave, Samuel, *A Century of Painters of the English School: With Critical Notices of Their Works, and An Account of the Progress of Art in England*. 2 vols. 2nd edition. London: Sampson Low & Co., 1890.

Reynolds, Graham, *British Watercolours*. London: H.M.S.O. and Victoria and Albert Museum, 1951.

Rienits, Rex, and Rienits, Thea, *Early Artists of Australia*. Sydney: Angus and Robertson, 1963.

Rosenberg, Jakob; Slive, Seymour, and Ter Kuile, E. H., *Dutch Art and Architecture, 1600 to 1800*. Harmondsworth: Penguin Books, 1966.

Ruskin, John, *Modern Painters*. Introduced by Lionel Cust. London: Everyman's Library, 1923. Vol. 1.

Sanborn, F. B., *Memoirs of Pliny Earle M.D.* Boston: Damrell & Ophan, 1898.

Smith, Bernard, *Australian Painting, 1788-1970*. Melbourne: Oxford University Press, 1971.

—— *European Vision and the South Pacific, 1768-1850: A Study in the History of Art and Ideas*. Oxford: Clarendon Press, 1960.

—— *Place, Taste and Tradition: A Study of Australian Art Since 1788*. Sydney: Ure Smith, 1945.

Spencer, Harold E., *A Picturesque Traveller on Tristan da Cunha*. Los Angeles: Occidental College, 1964.

'Augustus Earle: a Study of Early Nineteenth Century Travel Art and its Place in English Landscape and Genre Traditions.' Ph.D. thesis, Harvard, 1967.

'The Brisbane Portraits.' *Journal of the Royal Australian Historical Society* 52 (1966):1-9.

Sutton, Thomas, *The Daniells: Artists and Travellers*. London: Bodley Head, 1954.

Tute, Warren, *Cochrane: A Life of Admiral the Earl of Dundonald*. London: Cassell, 1965.

Ward, Russel, *The Australian Legend*. Melbourne: Oxford University Press, 1958.

Waterhouse, Ellis, *Painting in Britain 1530-1790*. London: Pelican, 1953.

Weidenhofer, Margaret, *The Convict Years: Transportation and the Penal System, 1788-1868*. Melbourne: Lansdowne, 1973.

Wilenski, Reginald, *English Painting*. London: Faber, 1933.

Willey, Basil, *The Eighteenth-Century Background: Studies on the Idea of Nature In the Thought of the Period*. Harmondsworth: Penguin Books, 1962.

Wood, Christopher, *Dictionary of Victorian Painters, With a Guide to Auction Prices, 300 Illustrations and Index to Artists' Monograms*. London: Antique Collectors' Club, 1971.